ROUTLEDGE LIBRARY EDITIONS:
EDUCATION

EDUCATIONAL REFORM

EDUCATIONAL REFORM
The Task of the Board of Education

FABIAN WARE

Volume 110

LONDON AND NEW YORK

First published in 1900

This edition first published in 2012
by Routledge
2 Park Square, Milton Park, Abingdon, Oxfordshire OX14 4RN

Simultaneously published in the USA and Canada
by Routledge
711 Third Avenue, New York, NY 10017

First issued in paperback 2014

Routledge is an imprint of the Taylor and Francis Group, an informa company

© 1900 Methuen & Co.

All rights reserved. No part of this book may be reprinted or reproduced or utilised in any form or by any electronic, mechanical, or other means, now known or hereafter invented, including photocopying and recording, or in any information storage or retrieval system, without permission in writing from the publishers.

Trademark notice: Product or corporate names may be trademarks or registered trademarks, and are used only for identification and explanation without intent to infringe.

British Library Cataloguing in Publication Data
A catalogue record for this book is available from the British Library

ISBN 13: 978-0-415-68927-4 (Volume 110)
ISBN 13: 978-0-415-75086-8 (pbk)

Publisher's Note
The publisher has gone to great lengths to ensure the quality of this reprint but points out that some imperfections in the original copies may be apparent.

Disclaimer
The publisher has made every effort to trace copyright holders and would welcome correspondence from those they have been unable to trace.

EDUCATIONAL REFORM

THE TASK OF THE BOARD OF EDUCATION

BY

FABIAN WARE

Vis consili expers mole ruit sua;
vim temperatam Di quoque provehunt
in majus; . . . .

METHUEN & CO.
36 ESSEX STREET, W.C.
LONDON
1900

NOTE

THE following chapters have been written in the hope that they may help to stimulate the interest of the public in the task to be undertaken by the new Board of Education. From secondary schoolmasters I ask for sympathetic, if severe, criticism of the work of a former member of their profession. Chapters IV. and IX. are mainly reproductions of articles which I recently contributed to the *Morning Post*. My thanks are due to the editor of that newspaper for kindly allowing me to use these articles for the present purpose.

F. W.

HAMPSTEAD, *December*, 1899

CONTENTS

CHAPTER I.
THE CLOSE OF AN EPOCH IN OUR EDUCATIONAL HISTORY

Forces promoting legislation on difficult and abstruse questions—Movement for organisation of education started by attack on local endowed schools—Endowed Schools Act, 1869, merely aimed at rearrangement of existing endowments—Elementary Education Act, 1870, a popular measure of social emancipation; hence machinery for its administration chiefly under popular control—Popular extension of higher education—Funds provided for technical instruction partly applied to this end—Higher-grade schools enter into competition with local endowed schools—Intellectuals press for organisation of authorities—Bryce Commission, 1894—Bill of 1896—Act of 1899, "in barest outline," aims at founding a national system   *Pages* 1-12

CHAPTER II.
REVIEW OF THE NATIONAL RESOURCES FOR SECONDARY EDUCATION

Elementary and technical education must benefit from reform of secondary—What is secondary education?—Answers to be obtained from its English development   .   .   .   13-15

The Public Schools.—Popular faith in public schools—Justified by their success in training of character—Essential that public schools should come under new Board—Willingness to place themselves at head of reform movement—Significant development of Head Masters' Conference, and Incorporated Association of Head Masters   16-21

Local Endowed Schools.—Their rise checked at Reformation—Boarding schools and day schools both essential—The term "Grammar School"—Confiscation of endowments at Reformation; directly and indirectly cause of present insufficiency—Failure of Charity Commissioners in better distribution of endowments—Local endowed schools and public schools have common origin and had common ideals—These ideals partly crushed in former by poverty—Costly demands of modern education—Its wider aims—Instruction in science—Modern sides of many local endowed schools subsidised by Science and Art Department, representing science *as opposed* to literature—Baneful results thus arising from want of organisation in central authority—Delicate task before new department for secondary education . . . . *Pages* 21–33

Private Schools.—Private enterprise a stimulating rivalry to Government agency—Duty of State to protect individual from educational fraud and imposture—Preparatory schools a necessary complement of public school system—*Raison d'être* of private schools: nurseries of methods and laboratories for experiment—Value of competition depends greatly on nature of award—Oxford and Cambridge locals and College of Preceptors' examinations not a test of educational efficiency—Such a test urgently needed, demanded by head masters . 34–39

Girls' Schools.—Great increase in supply of secondary education for girls—Change of aim in women's education intellectually and physically—Women are the authorities in England on education of women—Improved status of women teachers—Women's counsel indispensable to Board of Education—Reasons for great part played by private enterprise in education of girls . 39–44

Wanted, a Census and Criterion of Efficiency.—Parliamentary return of secondary schools—Valuable statistics; but only deal with quantity, not quality—Inspection alone can determine quality—Therefore Board must inspect; as existing supply must be utilised as far as efficient . . . 44–46

CHAPTER III.

HIGHER TECHNICAL EDUCATION
COMMERCIAL AND INDUSTRIAL

Example of municipal supply of technical education—Surprise of a municipal committee on visiting Germany—Responsibility and significant inconsistency of Science and Art Department—Technical education in Prussia based on secondary education—Prussian secondary schools—Popular confusion in England as to foundations of technical education—Industrial and commercial sciences must be taught as other sciences—Pressing need for higher technical education—*Note* on use of term "technical" 47–55

CONTENTS

CHAPTER IV.
AGRICULTURAL EDUCATION

Agricultural education in Denmark; success in butter-making depends on sound general education—Need of training of intelligence in rural schools—How to arouse interest in nature, and thus counteract attractions of town life—Teaching of history to explain relation of agriculture to national supremacy—Educational functions of Board of Agriculture to be taken over by Board of Education—Past educational work of Board of Agriculture—Rural evening continuation schools . . *Pages* 56-66

CHAPTER V.
ORGANISATION OF THE BOARD OF EDUCATION

Blunders due to past organisation expressed in terms of colonial government — Precedent established by government of India: that special cases demand special treatment, *i.e.* separate departments—Common educational aim of three branches must be represented in central organisation—Responsibility of permanent secretary—Peculiar difficulties of secondary assistant secretary—Need of diplomacy, not coercion, in dealing with secondary schools—Dread of traditions of Education Department—Influence of competent secondary assistant secretary on Universities—Harmony essential between three departments—Mutual influence they may exercise . . . 67-78

CHAPTER VI.
THE CONSULTATIVE COMMITTEE

Not an entirely new feature in central government—Relation of Indian Council to Indian Office and Parliament—How far analogous to that of Consultative Committee to Board of Education and Parliament—Reasons for greater influence of latter with Parliament—Functions of Consultative Committee —Registration—Selection of inspectors—Dismissal of assistant masters—Significance of new organ in home government—Composition of committee, not a pedantocracy nor a popular representative assembly—Sympathy with secondary assistant secretary essential **79-87**

CONTENTS

CHAPTER VII.
THE REGISTRATION OF TEACHERS

Need of training of secondary teachers—Buying teachers in the cheapest market—Large proportion of teachers without university degree—Economic cause: University scholarships and the rich—A register of teachers essential—Other qualifications besides scholarship needed—How to register these qualifications—Register of schools must first be formed . *Pages* 88–94

CHAPTER VIII.
THE INSPECTION AND EXAMINATION OF SECONDARY SCHOOLS

Registration of teachers and schools presupposes inspection—Examination must be supplemented by inspection—Preliminary inspection for formation of registers—Higher objects of inspection—Schools of unquestionable efficiency suffer from examination test—Civil Service and University Scholarship examinations—State leaving examination undesirable—Inspection alone can test education as distinct from instruction—Qualifications of inspectors—Their mission active, not passive—Assistant Masters' Association and inspection 95–104

CHAPTER IX.
THE BOARD OF EDUCATION AND WELSH SECONDARY SCHOOLS

Secondary education already organised in Wales—History of the national educational revival in Wales—Reasons for keeping Welsh and English secondary education distinct—Experience of certain members of Charity Commission indispensable to Board of Education—What is meant by inspection in Wales . 105–113

CHAPTER X.
LOCAL AUTHORITIES FOR SECONDARY EDUCATION

Opposition to spread of democratic local government—Failure of Government to solve problem of local authorities for secondary education—Indispensable conditions for entrusting secondary education to local authorities—Immediate need of "machines

CONTENTS

for raising and employing money"—Technical and elementary local authorities—School Boards not compatible with fundamental principles of local government—The future of local government lies with system re-established in 1888 and 1894—Objections to area smaller than that of county or county borough—Power of local authorities—Inspection must be carried out by central authority—County Councils cannot be allowed to use education for experiments in local government . . . . . *Pages* 114-123

CHAPTER XI.

THE NATION'S OPPORTUNITY

Foundations of empire : character and wealth—Each of little value alone in the modern race for national existence—Formation of character chief aim of past education of governing classes—Before franchise was extended somewhat similar education should have been bestowed on lower classes—Act of 1870 established education cut off from influence of schools educating governing classes; since latter were allowed to remain outside State system—They must now be brought into the State system ; and influence those already there ; and be influenced by them to train wealth-producing faculties—Greater stress must be laid on training of intelligence in secondary schools—Secondary and elementary schools must co-operate in providing sure foundation for technical education—The great need of "harmony or oneness"—Summary of what the Board of Education must do in the immediate future 124-139

THE NATIONAL SYSTEM OF SCHOOLS[1]

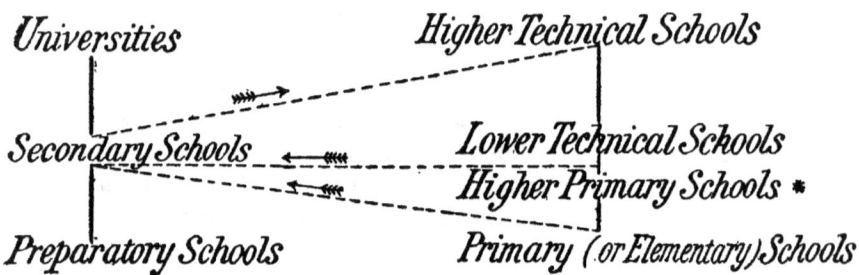

* *Commonly called Higher Grade Schools.*

[1] Designed to show the "educational ladder," and omitting varieties of schools difficult to classify; in the class Preparatory Schools, for instance, are included the lower forms of many boys' and girls' schools.

EDUCATIONAL REFORM

CHAPTER I.

THE CLOSE OF AN EPOCH IN OUR EDUCATIONAL HISTORY

IN spite of everything that has been done in this country to give all classes of the people a share in the government, it is no unusual thing to find an important measure, which neither excites widespread interest nor commands general sympathy, receiving the sanction of Parliament. And it is probably owing, in no small degree, to this fact and its underlying causes, that English democracy has been able in the past to steer clear, with apparent ease, of no few of those shoals on which foreign democracies have more than once been wrecked, and which they must often strain every nerve to avoid. Some little interest, representing an insignificant minority of the people, and possessing neither influence nor weight, will be attacked and threatened with extinction. Its claim for consideration will reach the ears of a small group of thoughtful men and women, who, free from the cares and responsibilities of public life, are ever watching over the destinies of the nation, and are endowed with a clearer vision along the path of progress than their fellows. Such persons individually often suffer the fate which is reserved for all those who are ahead of their times; but, united around a common cause, restrained by all the influences of association, they form an irresistible progressive force, acting slowly but surely. When once they are persuaded that the claims of the interest in question affect the larger interests of the nation, that its suppression represents a definite loss to the forces in the direction in which national progress can alone mean prosperity, they will support these claims with their combined intelligence and influence.

Happily for us their influence is not to be estimated by their numbers or by those material advantages which are so highly prized by the modern world. Nor is it a merely negative influence, arousing the passionate opposition encountered by their kindred spirits, the Intellectuals of France. It is to be measured by the confidence still possessed by the people of this country in the sincerity of their patriotism, a confidence that will leave in the hands of the English Intellectuals the solution of problems too abstruse for a public which, for the most part, is fully occupied with the struggle for existence. Their influence is further shown by the ease with which they collect, from all parties in Parliament, a small group to represent their views and to adapt their solutions to the practical exigencies of politics. No more striking example of its power has been afforded during recent years than the passing of the Board of Education Act of 1899.

To start at the commencement of the movement which has carried this measure through Parliament, we find the small and generally ignored interest attacked. Not more than thirty years ago the majority of the endowed schools, scattered over the land, were merely regarded as offering a makeshift secondary education for those parents who could not afford to send their children away to the great public schools. Treated with a not always unmerited disdain by the more fortunate and better equipped educational institutions, they rarely commanded the respect of the people, and were often objects of a scarcely veiled hostility. That they did little of their own free will to adapt themselves to the religious views or practical needs of the districts in which they were situated, and that, while frequently unable to rise to a state of efficiency, they tried to maintain an attitude of dignified isolation, of social and intellectual superiority to their surroundings, were in themselves sufficient causes for the want of sympathy evinced towards them by the public. And yet, looking back over the movement which led to the Board of Education Act, it must be admitted that it was the attack on these schools which first gave it its impetus.

To substantiate this assertion I must revert to the years 1869 and 1870, when two educational Acts of the first importance were passed. It is necessary, for reasons which will appear, to lay special emphasis on the fact that a negligible length of time separated the passing of these two Acts. The former, the Endowed Schools Act, dealt with that class of schools to which I have just alluded. Its object was defined as that "of promoting their greater efficiency, and of carrying into effect the main designs of the founders thereof, by putting a liberal education within the reach of children of all classes." Commissioners were appointed to administer this Act, but in 1874 their functions were transferred to the Charity Commissioners, whom we may therefore, to avoid confusion, regard as the central authority controlling these schools. The point to be noticed here in connection with this Act is that endowed schools, with very few exceptions, such as Cathedral Schools, were compelled to allow exemption, without any attendant disadvantage, from religious services or lessons to any scholars whose parents or guardians claimed this right. Thus the public hostility to these schools, in so far as it was based on religious grounds, was in a great degree allayed.

The latter of these Acts, the Elementary Education Act, was in every sense of the word a popular measure. It aimed at providing, for the first time in the history of England and Wales, equal educational opportunities within certain limits of age for the children of all classes. Moreover, it represented a compromise, in the interests of social progress, between the various religious forces which were contending for the control of the elementary education of all or of special denominations; and it was only after a protracted and weary struggle, which has had the unfortunate effect of causing Parliament since then to fight shy of educational questions, that public opinion insisted on the removal of the religious obstacles to an adequate supply of elementary schools.

We have already become so accustomed to regard the elementary education of all classes of the people as a matter of course, that it is difficult for some of us, who cannot remember the long travail that preceded the birth of this measure, to appreciate the momentous social changes which it brought about. The right of education thus bestowed was a link in the great chain of emancipation which began with the extinction of serfdom, and will end in the establishment of absolute equality of opportunity.

So clearly did this Act mark a triumph of the people, as distinct from the privileged classes, that it is not surprising that they were made directly responsible for the supply of the new schools. Hence arose the School Boards to furnish, to a great extent, the requisite funds. No surer means could have been devised for encouraging public interest in elementary education than that of entrusting it in a great measure to popularly elected local authorities, and of thus allowing the people who provide money for this purpose in their own districts not only to have a more direct responsibility as to its expenditure, but a clearer insight into the relation between expenditure and result than can possibly be obtained through the complicated system of aid from the national exchequer.

It is not at this point a question of the principles of local self-government. I wish merely to draw attention to the very different kinds of impetus that were given respectively to secondary and elementary education by two Acts, passed, one might almost say, simultaneously. The former was placed under the control of a central authority, so curtailed in its resources that, at the best, but slow progress could be made and but totally inadequate funds applied to the perfecting of the work entrusted to its care. The latter was committed to the charge of a strong central authority, on the one hand, with every facility for benefiting from the national taxes; on the other, to local authorities, which not only had the power of drawing, practically to an unlimited extent, on the local rates, but which brought popular enthusiasm to bear on the promotion of popular education.

The Schools Inquiry Commission, reporting on secondary education in 1867, remarked, "Every arrangement which fosters the interest of the people in the schools, which teaches the people to look on the schools as their own, which encourages them to take a share in the management, will do at least as much service as the wisest advice and the most skilful administration." If it is safe to draw any comparison between secondary and elementary education, the truth of this statement is borne out by the manner in which the people have been led by the Act of 1870 to look on the elementary schools as their own, and to regard the School Board as the power which would enable them to procure whatever education a majority might demand; while, on the other side, the smaller endowed schools under the control of the Charity Commissioners have never enjoyed popular favour in the same degree.

The result might have been foreseen. The people rapidly extended their claim for educational opportunities until they were no longer satisfied with the elementary education provided by the grants of the Education Department and by the rates levied on behalf of the School Boards. They demanded something higher. It can hardly be denied, looking back on the events of the last ten years, that a point was reached some time ago at which this demand became so pronounced that it was dangerous any longer to refuse to adopt the recommendation of the Schools Inquiry Commission, and to entrust secondary education to the good-will of the people. If the demand for higher education was irresistible, and the sequel has shown that it was, it clearly became the duty of the State to guide it in its realisation along the safest path towards national welfare.

Germany and France—to mention only two other European nations—had already solved the same problem, so that we were neither without example nor warning; and Englishmen of undisputed authority had for years held up both before us. A considerable period of time must elapse, however, before the eye of history can be focussed on all the scattered events of the last ten years and clearly perceive the causes which led to the neglect of a solution of the problem as it presented itself in England. At the present moment we can do no more than record facts and draw broad conclusions.

As the popular demand for higher education entered the cooling atmosphere of practical politics, it naturally crystallised around the only centre of educational attraction possessed by the people—the Board School. To add an upper department to this institution appeared the most direct means of bringing higher education under popular control. The one difficulty was to find the requisite money. If there had been no way of obtaining this, it may be taken for granted that public opinion would have compelled Parliament to discover, several years ago, a solution of the difficulty, and to have built up a national system, in so far as secondary and elementary education were concerned. But there was one source from which money might be drawn without further legislation.

The need of increased scientific and artistic knowledge among the industrial classes had long been recognised, and the Technical Instruction Acts of 1889 and 1891 had provided facilities for the spread of this knowledge in no grudging spirit. The recent growth in England of technical instruction is, in some respects, one of the most satisfactory chapters in the history of educational progress during the last half of the present century. Rarely has such earnestness of purpose been brought to bear on the solution of a purely educational question. But, remaining as it did in unchallenged possession of the attention which the people devoted to higher education, it is not to be wondered at that the effort which was put forward on behalf of technical instruction should have given a strong bias to the rising popular demand referred to. Neither is it surprising that the people should have turned at first for guidance, which was not forthcoming from other quarters, to the many earnest men and women who were advocating the claims of technical instruction in all parts of the country.

But to consider only the practical side of the question, which always appeals so strongly to Englishmen. The money placed at the disposal of the Science and Art Department, under the Acts to which I have alluded above, for the promotion of technical instruction, offered the only means of satisfying what had become the most important condition of the new demand, namely, that higher as well as elementary education should be directly under popular control. For if upper departments were added to the Board Schools, by bestowing technical instruction they might claim a share of the money thus provided. This, in a few words, is the history of the foundation of higher-grade schools.

How far the School Boards have been legally justified in further strengthening these schools by applying the rates to their maintenance is a question which does not concern us here. It is merely necessary to notice that by the establishment of higher-grade schools very formidable rivals were raised up to threaten the existence of the smaller endowed schools, rivals which were all the more dangerous, not only because they were supported partly by local funds and represented a new type of higher education which appealed strongly to the popular mind, but because they were under the direction of a department which was in a position to give them ample financial assistance, and eager to do so, from a sincere, though obstinate and too one-sided, devotion to an educational theory which, in more enlightened circles, has already fallen into desuetude. A contest between the higher-grade schools, thus supported, and the smaller endowed schools, controlled by the Charity Commissioners, could but have ended in disaster for the latter; and it should be remembered that such disaster meant the extinction of that traditional type of secondary education which these schools had, very feebly in some cases it must be confessed, represented.

Such was the position of affairs when the group of thoughtful men and women, referred to at the beginning of this chapter, took up the cause of secondary education to which they were first attracted by the cry of distress proceeding from the smaller endowed schools.

It was not that the new type of higher education was based on totally wrong principles, nor that the old was suited to modern requirements. Each had its good as well as its bad points; the traditions of the one had to be adapted to the modern spirit of the other. But such a fusion of educational principles could only be brought about by well-organised authorities, in which all interests were duly represented. However able and sincere the ruling spirits in the Science and Art Department, its very constitution, necessitated by the objects which it was established to attain, was bound to give it a strong prejudice against the older methods and principles of English education; and in a contest with the Charity Commission, the grievously handicapped champion of the endowed schools, its power was irresistible. It is chiefly due to the wise forbearance of some of its leading officials that it did not take even greater advantage of these powers.

It will be evident that the educational issues involved were of too abstruse a nature to excite any popular enthusiasm; and had it not been for the persistent efforts of the Intellectuals they would never have been forced on the attention of Parliament. But, a small group of members having once been interested in the matter, the question soon entered the sphere of practical politics.

As departments of the central government, with their local counterparts, existed for the support and encouragement of elementary and technical education, the natural course appeared to be to appoint similar bodies to preside over secondary education. The Bryce Commission, appointed in 1894, and particularly remarkable for the fact that it was the first Royal Commission to include women among its members, recommended in some detail the steps which should be taken for the creation of such authorities.

Warned, however, of the immense difficulties which stood in the way of some of these proposals, by the fate of the Bill of 1896, Lord Salisbury's Government perceived that the question of secondary education could not be dealt with apart from the wider one of national education; that for separate central authorities, with their respective satellites, to preside over the three branches of education, which were now to come under the supervision of the State, would simply result in a continuation of overlapping and in a keener strife; that for the due success of a national system it is essential that, if a distinct local authority is necessary for each of the three branches of education, to it should be assigned a clearly defined sphere of influence, and that in any case harmonious and concurrent action must first be assured among the different departments of the central authority.

The Board of Education Act is the outcome of this new view as to the best means of promoting the interests of secondary education. The measure itself is, it must be confessed, in the barest outline, and, as an able critic has remarked, "everything will depend on the development of its suggestions and the spirit in which it is administered."[1]

[1] *The Educational Systems of Great Britain and Ireland*, p. xxxii. note 1, by GRAHAM BALFOUR, M.A. (Clarendon Press, 1898.)

CHAPTER II.

REVIEW OF THE NATIONAL RESOURCES FOR SECONDARY EDUCATION

FROM the foregoing sketch of the causes which led to the passing of the Board of Education Act, it will be evident that the chief work before the Board is the organisation of secondary education, not as an isolated branch, but in such a way as to bring it into its proper relation to the national system which must be developed. It is only by keeping this main object steadily in view that the Board can succeed in the very delicate and complicated task before it. To make the supply of secondary education adequate, and gradually to raise its standard of efficiency throughout the country, will demand no small labour and patience. The utmost skill and tact, and the widest knowledge of our educational system, will be required if this is to be done in such a way that technical education will also directly benefit; and if the supporters of primary education are to be persuaded that it is to their immediate interest to remove all inferior teaching and misapprehension of aims from our secondary schools, and to confer on them such stability and definiteness of purpose, that elementary education will, if I may use the figure, no longer have to attempt to prepare its brightest intellects for their passage through a chaotic and limitless region, presenting ever-changing conditions of atmosphere and climate.

The first step, therefore, which the Board will have to take is an eminently practical one: that of acquiring reliable information as to the existing supply, nature, and quality of secondary education in this country. In a collection of essays recently published an attempt has been made, with considerable success, to give an answer to the far from simple question, "What is Secondary Education?"[1] It will be necessary for the Board to discover a clear and decisive answer to this question before it is in a position to guide the future development of secondary education, or even to collect the information required.

There are two ways of obtaining such an answer. The first is by consulting the theory of education in its universal application; the second is by accepting the answer already given by the practical development of secondary schools in England during the last five hundred years, and by observing any failure of this development, in its highest phases, to meet modern English requirements. The latter is certainly the way which will recommend itself to any body of practical Englishmen inheriting our traditional modes of thought and action.

A comparison of the answers thus obtained with that offered by the secondary systems of some foreign countries, more particularly Germany, will be useful;

---

[1] *What is Secondary Education? Essays on the Problems of Organisation.* Edited by R. P. SCOTT, M.A., LL.D. (Rivingtons.)

but it should not be entered upon without a thorough appreciation of the dangers involved. The fate of Matthew Arnold's brilliant efforts in this direction will be a warning to the few scattered individuals who have not yet learnt that, if the future progress of England is to depend more and more on education—that is to say on the cultivation of our inherited qualities—and if progress, according to the teaching of modern science, can only be a process of evolution from the inherited onwards and upwards, it is essential that this education should be English in its outward form and inward spirit, in its aims and its methods; in short, that it must, at each stage, be a resultant of forces acting within the English nation, and having as their source the English mind and conscience.[1]

The secondary schools of England are popularly divided into four groups—the great public schools, the local endowed schools,[2] private schools, and girls' schools. It will be well to glance briefly at the supply, nature, and quality of the secondary education provided by each group.

[1] As a striking example of the modern appreciation of this fact, compare with MATTHEW ARNOLD'S *Universities and Higher Schools in Germany*, Mr. MICHAEL E. SADLER'S paper on "Problems in Prussian Secondary Education for Boys, with Special Reference to Similar Questions in England," *Special Reports on Educational Subjects*, vol. ii. (Eyre and Spottiswoode, 1898.)

[2] More popularly known as grammar schools, from the most important feature of the group.

THE PUBLIC SCHOOLS.

It may be said, with very slight exaggeration, that it is the ambition of every English parent, who can afford to furnish his sons with secondary education, to send them to one of the public schools. The average Englishman will tell you, unhesitatingly, that the best of schools is Eton, and that there has never been so great a schoolmaster as Dr. Arnold of Rugby. A belief in the public schools is deeply rooted in the English nation; and though the establishment of the Board of Education has excited but little popular enthusiasm, it must not be thought that public opinion would remain quiescent were an attempt to be made to create a new type of secondary education for the people, which was neither a continuation of, nor influenced by, the development of our public schools during the last five hundred years.

It is not the still existing, if lessened, respect for social rank which underlies this belief in the public schools; that may have something to do with it, and may strengthen the desire of the lower classes for a similar type of education for their own children. But the truth is to be found in the popular conviction that these schools, with all their faults, make it their first object to awaken in their pupils those moral qualities which have, in the popular opinion, raised the English character above that of neighbouring nations. And this conviction has been strengthened of late years by the knowledge that many foreigners, whose educational systems are considered to be in some respects superior to our own, have studied these schools in order to learn how they have solved the problem of the training of character—a problem which has baffled so many foreign educationists of world-wide renown.

The student of education must confess that this popular conviction is well founded. He must admit that the public schools have discovered unconsciously, or rather instinctively, how to reconcile school discipline with that freedom of individual development which modern science teaches us is one of the most essential factors in human progress. On the other hand, none would be rash enough to assert that all the masters in these schools allow sufficient freedom to the development of the intelligence in particular; nor that they invariably place knowledge before their pupils in its most attractive form and inspire them with that enthusiastic spirit of inquiry, that many-sided intellectual interest, which is the final proof of unimpeachable methods of instruction. This is also popularly recognised by the public, and we hear complaints from all sides that the boys in these schools might learn more, and acquire a greater taste for knowledge, and a cast of intelligence better adapted to the stress of modern competition. And yet, in spite of these defects, such importance do the English attach to the training of character in secondary education, that any increase of national prosperity—that is to say, any alleviation of the pressure on the incomes of parents—invariably results in an addition to the numbers of the pupils attending the great public schools.

C

It must not be imagined, however, that during the last fifty years these schools have been allowed to persist without check in methods of education and courses of study suited only to an earlier stage of civilisation. Direct interference of the State has removed many of their abuses, and widened their curricula beyond the range of an exclusively classical education. But the point deserving especial notice is that there is something in the atmosphere of these schools which defies definition and cannot be reduced to any educational formula; and it is precisely this which meets with the approval of the English people. Its results on the men who have spent their boyhood and youth under its influence are equally difficult to define, but yet are recognised by Englishmen and foreigners alike as of the very highest moral value. If public opinion were to be allowed complete freedom of expression in the organisation which is to be undertaken by the Board, there is no doubt that this spirit, which has breathed through our public schools since the foundation of Winchester, would be accounted that which is of most worth in English secondary education. It would be recognised as the essential English characteristic which must form the basis of the improved curricula—adopted by some other nations as the courses of study best calculated to prepare a boy for life in the modern world—if they are to be framed with due regard to the traditional English influences. For it is English influences which have promoted English progress, and which can alone aid us to work out our own salvation, and to avoid the dangers in the confusion and pessimism threatening some of our neighbours with moral atrophy.

To foster this spirit in our public schools will be one of the highest and not the least difficult duties of the Board of Education, should they submit themselves to its control. Nay, more; the Board is directly responsible to the people for their coming under its control, in accordance with the definite undertaking into which they entered with the country during the passing of the Board of Education Act. There is not the least doubt that they will adhere strictly to this promise, unless the Board obliges them to act otherwise in defence of that very freedom on which their vitality depends. Fortunately, the interest of the nation to preserve the best traditions of our public schools, and to spread them throughout the whole of secondary education, coincides with the private interest of these schools themselves. For it may be observed from their present attitude and from the policy that they have pursued during recent years in connection with other schools, that the public schools have fully appreciated the necessity of placing themselves at the head of the reform of secondary education, if they would not be abandoned to the fate which befell kindred institutions in Germany.

One striking example of this is afforded by the action of the Head Masters' Conference. This most conservative of all educational bodies has gradually widened its circle so as to admit the representatives of many schools which do not rank in the popular estimation among the great public schools. But the reciprocal advantages of such action have been great, for while the qualification for admission to the Conference has been the possession of, in some degree, a common educational ideal with that of the public school, the schools thus represented have not only gained inestimable benefits from the opportunity afforded them of discussing this ideal with those who have most nearly attained its realisation, but have, on their side, contributed no less to pedagogical progress by bringing to the Conference a practical knowledge of the educational requirements of the modern commercial and industrial world. I refer particularly to the greater number of the local endowed schools. It is perhaps on this account that the opinions of the Head Masters' Conference on the problems of secondary education always command respect, and carry unequalled weight with those who believe that progress is best secured by a succession of compromises between the supporters of tradition and the representatives of the modern spirit.

The Board of Education will run no risk of being in advance of public opinion if it grants all the demands of the Head Masters' Conference; it has at any rate one extremely useful lesson to learn from this body, namely, that it is impossible to draw any hard and fast line of demarcation between the different grades of secondary schools, seeing that the most conservative among them have been led to admit the kinship of an increasing number of apparently inferior institutions. The same fact might be inferred from the growth of the Incorporated

Association of Head Masters, which, starting nearly ten years ago with the head masters of public[1] secondary schools who were excluded from the Conference, has now been joined by more than forty members of the latter body.

LOCAL ENDOWED SCHOOLS.

So far we have been merely deducing certain principles as to the course of action to be pursued by the Board of Education, rather than establishing a just cause for its interference in the domain of secondary education. The latter will plainly appear from a brief consideration of the position of local endowed schools and the two other classes referred to.

It is hardly necessary to remark that the majority of the great public schools do not supply only, or even chiefly, their own localities, but draw by far the greater number of their pupils from different parts of the country. In this connection should be noted the suppression of many local schools at the Reformation, for the exposure of which we are almost exclusively indebted to Mr. Arthur Leach's gift of patient research. There is little doubt that the check thus given to the natural development of secondary education, of a very high type, in the various centres of population — a check the force of which may be estimated by a comparison between the proportion of secondary schools to the population in our own days and in the years

---

[1] The term in this sense being taken to mean any school which is administered under a definite form of public or corporate control.

immediately preceding the Reformation—must be reckoned as a very important factor in the rise of our non-local public schools.

Whatever the causes, however, it must now be recognised that the custom of sending children away from their homes to boarding schools has become, for a certain section of the people, one of those national habits which are second nature. To eliminate such a custom in a nation like Germany, at a time when its various scattered forces were uniting in a common national aim, is a very different thing from stamping it out, were it possible to do so, in a country which has for long attained to a very high stage of national development, and whose future progress must depend on the adaptation of acquired habits to the demands arising from the bewilderingly rapid advance of civilisation.

On the other hand, while it is perhaps best that a small fraction of the public should continue to send their children away to boarding schools, it must be remembered that, in our large towns and the immediately surrounding districts, by far the greater number of that section of the population, which it is commonly agreed cannot dispense with secondary education, are either unable to afford the fees of boarding schools, or prefer that their children's education should be carried on under their daily supervision. The local endowed schools are still the chief means of satisfying this need.

It is outside the scope of the present work to trace all the causes which have stunted the growth of these schools. One of the most serious has been referred to above; as for the rest, some of their effects can alone be noticed. It is a significant fact that, while the term "grammar school" now conveys to the popular mind the idea of a local endowed school only, formerly it was applied to both Winchester and Eton, to take two of the most striking examples of its earlier meaning.[1] Indeed, many of the existing grammar schools are hardly less venerable than these two famous colleges, and when founded were intended to —and most of them for a long time did—give precisely the same education; and, what is perhaps still more interesting, many of them were endowed with the distinct purpose of providing free, that is to say gratuitous,[2] education.

The confiscation of a number of these endowments by the Crown at the time of the Reformation was in itself sufficient to shake the security, as an investment for the money of future benefactors, of the gratitude and welfare of posterity. But the system of endowments, making all allowance for the general increase in the value of property, could only continue to meet the educational requirements of the people so long as new benefactors arose in proportion to the growth of the population, and so long as old endowments were adapted to its displacement.

To pass on to our own times. It is beyond question that, totally insufficient as existing endowments are to provide an adequate supply of secondary

---

[1] In some cases (*e.g.* Birmingham) the term is now confined to the offshoots of the local endowed school, which in its turn is called the "high school."

[2] Cf. ARTHUR F. LEACH, *English Schools at the Reformation*, pp. 110–114. (Archibald Constable and Co., 1896.)

education, a better distribution would cause them to go a great deal further than they do. This was fully emphasised by the Bryce Commission; but it is poor consolation for the present state of affairs to read in their report: "We were reminded that it has been said that the Endowed Schools Acts made it possible to turn a boys' school in Northumberland into a girls' school in Cornwall, and it is not improbable that the very greatness of the power may largely account for the notorious inability of the Charity Commissioners to exercise it."[1] The Board of Education being able to take over this power, under the Act of 1899, will be held responsible for exercising it in the future; much will depend on their energy and ability in this respect. It may be true that, with a few notable exceptions such as the King Edward's Schools, Birmingham, the most richly endowed schools are often the least efficient; but yet in many ways poverty has been a great stumbling-block and source of evil to the majority of these schools.

The local endowed school and the public school have, it may again be noticed, a common origin. It is therefore not surprising that they possess many features in common. The points of similarity between the two types have been maintained by several means, chiefly through their connection with the Universities and the preference shown by the grammar schools for masters who have been educated in the public schools. Such masters invariably take for their models the educational methods from which they

[1] Vol. i. p. 176.

themselves had benefited. We therefore find many grammar schools enjoying all the benefits of the games, and as far as possible (most of them being day schools) of the social and corporate life of the public schools; and thirty years ago the curricula of both were to all intents and purposes identical.

Now there is a point here which is well worthy of notice. Whatever abuses had been introduced into our system of secondary education, and the Schools Inquiry Commission exposed many in 1867, formerly secondary education meant but one thing for rich and poor, for the higher and lower social classes alike. Its ideal was culture; it was a preparation for the University, where the gentleman finished off the course of education which was considered best fitted to qualify him for the position he would be called upon to occupy in the country. Its motto was "Manners makyth Man," and the idea of its becoming a preliminary course of apprenticeship for various trades and professions hardly entered into the heads of its guardians. And when the democratic spirit first began to move in this country, of all the desires which it stirred none was worthier than that of obtaining for all children the same education as was given to those of the privileged classes. It was a desire which found an echo in the hearts of true educators, and brought hope to many a schoolmaster who had been toiling against the insufficient endowment of his school in his endeavours to realise this ideal.

It is not difficult to understand the feelings with which the Endowed Schools Act of 1869 must have inspired many masters of local endowed schools. Here was a body set up by the Government with full power to reorganise educational endowments; to transfer them from localities in which, owing to the displacement of population, they were no longer useful, to those where they were sorely needed; to supplement them by others originally destined to purposes now obsolete; to make schemes for the administration of these endowments, and to inspect the schools in order to see that the greatest possible use was made of them in education and instruction. It appeared as if at last the grammar schools in our large centres of population were once more to take up the work for which they were founded, and to give to as many of the people as possible the opportunity of obtaining that culture which has been considered indispensable to our governing classes.

That the Charity Commissioners have failed to give full force to the provisions of this Act; that the progress they have made in the reorganisation of endowments is in no way commensurate with the number of years which they have devoted to the task; that many of the abuses and anachronisms of 1869 still exist to-day, must be attributed mainly to the fact that no serious attempt has been made to bestow on them the machinery and the means necessary for the great work committed to their charge. We consequently find that, with very few exceptions, the grammar schools in our large towns are prevented by want of funds from maintaining a high standard of efficiency. They have long ago given up attempting to provide only free educa-

NATIONAL RESOURCES

tion, and have been obliged to satisfy popular feeling by offering a certain number of scholarships. Neither can they depend to any great extent on fees; for the competition of private schools, and more recently of higher-grade schools, compels them to reduce these fees to the lowest possible point. And even if a grammar school succeeded twenty years ago in maintaining a certain standard of efficiency with the funds at its disposal, it by no means follows that it is able to do so to-day.

It must be remembered that secondary education, even if, or rather because, its main object is the imparting of culture, must adapt itself to the advance of modern civilisation. Literary studies alone were doubtless sufficient for attaining this object, when the forces of nature were but little understood and their action was controlled by man to no appreciable extent. But in our own days things are very different. Every year adds to the list of natural forces which have been brought under the sway of man; the conditions of national life are as different from those of our grandfathers as theirs were from those of their ancestors in the time of the Renaissance; even our mental life is affected to an incalculable degree by the part which has been played by science in forming our environment. Our educationists are slowly but surely beginning to see that the true aim of education is the adaptation of the child to its spiritual, physical, and mental environment, and that this adaptation can only be achieved by bringing it gradually under the influence of those forces which have moulded the environment.[1] To omit to instruct any modern boy in the eternal truths of science is no less dangerous to his mental development than to bring him up in ignorance of the world's literature, that stately storehouse of the thoughts of man, containing forces to propel the world up the spiral path of progress and above all to check the centrifugal tendencies of speculation.

Such a theoretical explanation of the right of science to a place in the curriculum of every secondary school may not appeal to the practical minds of Englishmen, but their common sense has long ago brought them to a similar conclusion. The fitting up of laboratories and the provision of apparatus represent no small expense; and when the poorer grammar schools were convinced that they must teach science, or succumb to outside competition, the question was where to find the necessary funds.

It is here that we first notice in any marked degree the baneful results of the attempt of the State to regulate education by piecemeal legislation. When the demand for instruction in science became urgent, and more particularly when the pressure of foreign competition gave to this demand a national importance, it was the undoubted duty of the State to see that it was met. It did so by establishing a strong central department with subordinate local authorities, and by placing at their disposal a considerable amount of money. But it took no pains

---

[1] Cf. NICHOLAS MURRAY BUTLER, *The Meaning of Education.* (Macmillan and Co., 1898.)

to inquire if there existed a central authority empowered to guard the interests of literary instruction against any undue encroachment of the newer learning. It is greatly to the credit of the Science and Art Department, or rather to the moderation of one more than any other of its chief officials, that it has not taken further advantage of its powers. But that very spirit of rivalry, and that natural desire to extend its sphere of control, which, when kept within due bounds, form a most useful stimulus to a Government department, were sure to entice the Science and Art Department to encroach on unclaimed territory. As has been pointed out in the opening chapter, the Charity Commissioners, who nominally presided over the whole field of education within the purview of the Endowed Schools Acts, were powerless to prevent such encroachments, or even to support the local endowed schools against the higher-grade schools, those rivals established by the Science and Art Department. The poorer grammar schools were enabled by the grants allocated in accordance with the syllabuses of the Science and Art Department, and determined by its inspectors, to satisfy the growing demand for instruction in science.[1]

Whatever means this department has adopted to safeguard the interests of literary instruction have proved a source of great danger to the educational traditions which these schools had for so long de-

---

[1] To aid me in my attempt to place this matter before the reader with the least possible confusion, I have omitted all allusion to instruction in art in this chapter.

fended. The syllabuses were extended so as to include every subject of instruction in secondary schools with the exception of Latin and Greek. The Science and Art Department thus established itself the central authority for these schools, in so far as their modern sides were concerned; but unfortunately it had been constituted solely for the purpose of encouraging instruction in Science and Art.

The history of the State control of secondary education up to this point hardly does credit to our vaunted powers of organisation. It is true that the schemes of the Charity Commissioners still determined what subjects might not be omitted from the curricula of local endowed schools. But the number of hours to be devoted to the teaching of these subjects, and the methods to be pursued, were left to the discretion of the head master and governors. This was originally a wise provision. But when the poorer grammar schools were compelled to turn to the Science and Art Department for financial assistance, they were obliged to accept its grants on its own terms. So that naturally the head master and governors had to agree to the division of hours approved by this department and to the methods sanctioned by its inspectors, so far as that part of the school was concerned which benefited directly from its grants.

Now, there is no possible exception to be taken to the principle that such control should be exercised by a State department which bestows, or regulates the bestowal of, grants. The principle is in itself admirable; insistence on the relative importance of various subjects, and wise and capable inspection, are two of the reforms which educationists have besought for secondary schools during the last thirty years. And nothing better can be desired than that both should be provided in the future with the same tact and energy as has occasionally characterised the Science and Art Department when acting in its own interests. But, again it must be repeated, this department was so constituted as to be qualified to supervise instruction in science and art alone. And not only this, but its *personnel*, including its inspectors, consisted, in its worthiest aspects, of men who had distinguished themselves in, or received their education during, the deplorable and bitter struggle between literature and science, at a time when these two branches of learning represented to their supporters the foundations of antagonistic beliefs as to the destiny of man.

We are now emerging from this struggle and have succeeded to a great extent in harmonising apparently rival forces. What M. Brunetière aptly described some four years ago as the renaissance of idealism marked the recovery from the uncertainty and confusion of this period of storm and stress. We may well ask, however, if the State, during this stage of transition, was true to its duty in allowing the entire secondary education of at least one half of the boys in poorer grammar schools to drift under the control of a department which stood as the champion of the scientific spirit. Was the State, or were even the governing classes, sufficiently persuaded of the finality of the belief of scientists to be justified in employing public money for the education of an important section of the population in this belief alone? What defence will history offer for the action of the State in thus, more through negligence than design, leaguing itself with the opponents, against the reformers, of the traditional ideals of English secondary education?

The results for those schools which have not been rich enough, or heroic enough, to resist the temptations of the Science and Art Department may be briefly summed up as follows. First, the modern sides of these schools have been transformed into "schools of science," in which what teaching there is of literary subjects is mainly controlled and inspected by the scientists of this department.

Secondly, no progress has consequently been made in the teaching of literary subjects. In the case of modern languages in particular the effect of this stagnation has been so strongly felt by the commercial classes as to raise a demand—based on the precedent establised by these schools of science—for schools of commerce within the sphere formerly recognised as sacred to secondary education.

Thirdly, the classical sides of such local endowed schools have gradually been cut adrift from modern influences, and have too often become the strongholds of that uncompromising literary spirit which is the deadliest foe of science. Thus a large section of the boys in these schools are being brought up in ignorance of, or at best with a superior indifference to, science and modern foreign literature—two of the most powerful forces in the modern environment. This is probably the most serious and dangerous

NATIONAL RESOURCES

of the results which I have summed up in these three divisions.

How the attention of a small body of thoughtful men and women was attracted to the perilous position of these schools, in face of the rivalry of higher-grade schools, has been pointed out in a former chapter. The Science and Art Department has certainly done much to save the local endowed schools from extermination by reproducing in them the educational tendencies of their other creations; but at what a cost! The most charitable view that can be taken of this is that it is a makeshift policy. The right policy will have to be determined by the Board of Education. It is a hopeful sign that Parliament has informally sanctioned the creation of a department for the control of secondary education, closely allied with the other departments, which it may be taken for granted will be composed exclusively neither of the representatives of science nor of those of literature, but will contain representatives of all those elements which go to make up an all-round secondary education adapted to modern English requirements.

From the slight sketch which has been given of some of the obstructions that have been placed in the way of the natural development of our local endowed schools, it will be seen that no branch of the new Board will require to bring deeper knowledge and sympathy, and greater tact, to bear on the work of organisation than this secondary department. This will become even more evident from a consideration of the very important position occupied in our educational system by private schools.

PRIVATE SCHOOLS.

A private school may be defined as one which is conducted by a private individual for his own pecuniary profit. It is true that there are here and there private schools which owe their existence to the educational enthusiasm of their owners, in which the idea of pecuniary profit is the last in the mind of the head master, and which have often introduced reforms of supreme value to educational progress. But these must necessarily prove the exception, for they are rarely self-supporting, and there is hardly the same willingness among the rich to subsidise educational experiments as in the days of Pestalozzi and Froebel. We may therefore, for the purpose of a general survey, adhere to our definition and admit the immediate conclusion to be drawn therefrom, namely, that a private school depends for its success on public favour.

It therefore represents that form of individual enterprise so dear to the minds of Englishmen; and it is wiser to recognise at the outset that, if only in order that a stimulating rivalry may be furnished to Government agency, it will command their support for many years to come, whatever extension of State control may follow the Board of Education Act. To point out that private schools of the immortal "Dotheboys Hall" type have existed, and still exist, in a modified form, will suggest the lines that State interference should follow, but will not be regarded as a sufficient excuse for placing all educational institutions under direct public control.

I have said that a private school depends for its success on public favour. That it is so, is the cause of much good, and perhaps of much evil. Whether the collective judgment of the public is invariably sound or not, it is certain that there is always a large number of people at the mercy of impostors. So true is this, that it has been found necessary to constitute a criminal offence the supply of food or other commodities in such a condition as will be detrimental to physical health. Indeed, it is a generally admitted principle, as far as any political principle can be said to be generally admitted nowadays, that it is the duty of the State to protect the individual from fraud and imposture. But for some reason, difficult to trace, the English people have not in the past considered it wise to extend this principle to the supply of secondary education, on which depends the mental, moral, spiritual, and, in a very large measure, the physical health of a vast number of children. In fact, had it not been for the protest of the teachers themselves, including the majority of private schoolmasters, the public would probably still submit, for many years to come, to the educational fraud and imposture perpetrated in every town. It is impossible to estimate the loss to the nation arising from the past indifference of many parents as to the conditions under which their children are educated.

To take only two of the worse forms of fraud and imposture. On the one hand, there are schools which pretend to furnish secondary education, while in the secrecy of their own classrooms they are providing nothing more than elementary education, of a type inferior to that of the Board schools and under far less satisfactory conditions. On the other hand, there are not a few, often conducted by men or women who should know better, which, with apparent intent to mislead, assume high-sounding titles, causing credulous parents to believe that within their walls their children may receive an education even higher than secondary.[1] To suppress such schools, or to compel them to reform, is not the least important work to be undertaken by the Board of Education. The means to be adopted must be dealt with later on.

But to turn to the better class of private schools. Those which are so well known as preparatory schools have grown up in the shadow of the great public schools, and are directly under their influence. Their curricula are regulated by the entrance examinations of the public schools; it is their duty to prepare for these examinations while adopting their methods of education and instruction to boys under the age of fifteen. Regarded as a class, they maintain a high standard of efficiency, and the worst that can be said of them is that until their reputation is established they are tempted to win it by over-working their pupils in order to gain success at these entrance examinations. So long as they are unable to prove their efficiency by satisfying other tests, this temptation will remain exceedingly strong. On

---

[1] "Gymnasium and University College," to take only one of many titles of the sort which may be seen in the streets of most of our towns.

the other hand, much good may be said of them; there are few brighter examples of English education than is offered by many of these schools, directed by men with brilliant qualifications, and themselves originally masters in public schools, who are inspired with the best English traditions, and who bring long experience, open minds, and great enthusiasm to bear on the education of young boys. That boys under a certain age require special educational treatment, which they cannot obtain in large schools, that many evils have arisen from massing boys of all ages together, even in the best regulated boarding schools, are sufficient causes for the existence of preparatory schools. But, at the same time, this intimate connection with the public schools, differentiating them from other private schools, must be the first consideration of the Board of Education when imposing any tests of their efficiency.

The great mass of private schools, while offering every possible variety, may be divided into boarding schools and day schools.[1] Generally speaking, the former, which draw their pupils from all parts of the country, aim at producing a cheaper type of public school. That is to say, they take the public school as their model, urged either by their own or the public conviction of its excellence. They thus supply a distinct national need, and besides this they may, and often do, contribute in a very special manner to educational progress. They are

[1] It is impossible in a sketch such as the present even to refer to minor varieties of any class of educational institution—though variety, as a most important factor in English education, cannot be ignored.

nurseries of new methods and laboratories for educational experiments. Not only are their head masters often educators of the highest ability, who are ever ready to adopt modern improvements, but they are incited by the spirit of competition to strain every nerve to excel their rivals.

This healthy emulation is in itself excellent, if only the meed of success is awarded by competent arbiters. But, unfortunately, that very section of the public which falls such an easy prey to educational impostors has no small voice in determining the awards of public favour on which these schools must depend. And yet this dependence on public favour must necessarily form the key to the private school problem. Eliminate it or take away the freedom of public choice, and the whole private school system must fall to the ground. What is wanted is some stable standard of measurement recognised by the public.

This has been offered by the examinations of outside bodies such as the Oxford University Delegacy, the Cambridge University Syndicate, and the College of Preceptors. But many head masters complain with justice, that, if the public are to judge of the relative efficiency of their schools by the number of pupils who satisfy the tests supplied by these bodies, they must abandon the higher aims of education in favour of that of preparing for written examinations, and that such preparation must degenerate into mere "cramming," a process which violates every educational precept. It is therefore not surprising that they should be among the foremost in desiring a true test of efficiency,

NATIONAL RESOURCES 39

established by the State, and consequently commanding the confidence of educationists and laity alike. No distinction can be drawn between the attitude in this respect of the head masters of either the day or boarding class of private schools.

The private day school has arisen, either owing to the inability of endowed schools to meet the requirements of a locality, or in response to the demand of certain parents for an education which satisfies definite religious or social conditions. Those which meet this demand will continue to exist, and, provided they are efficient, will contribute no little to the moral force and stamina of the nation. The former, however, will gradually cease to have any *raison d'être* in proportion as the local endowed schools grow and prosper under the fostering care of the Board of Education.

It is interesting to observe that 38·1 per cent. of the boys included in the Parliamentary Return of 1898 as receiving secondary education,* were to be found in private schools. In the case of girls, however, the numbers are far greater, rising to no less than 70·3 per cent.

Girls' Schools.

The education of girls is a subject which yearly claims an increasing share of public attention. Before 1864 there were only fourteen endowed secondary schools for girls in England and Wales; in 1895 there were about eighty, and considerably more than twice that number supported by various

* As to the value of these statistics *see* below, p. 45.

bodies of subscribers and companies, such as the Girls' Public Day Schools Company.[1]

The Report of the Schools Inquiry Commission, presented in 1867, did much to stimulate public interest in the education of girls; but there are deeper reasons to account for the extraordinary progress which has been made during the last thirty years.

The necessity for a large number of women, in the upper and middle classes, to gain an independent livelihood has steadily increased, and before it the aim of secondary education for girls has changed. The attainment of social accomplishments and the preparation for married life can no longer be regarded as its sole object. To look at this phase of the question from an eminently practical point of view, preparation for marriage fills much the same place in a girl's education as technical training in a boy's. To train all boys under the age of sixteen for a special trade or profession is, to say the least, unwise; for, considered from a purely educational standpoint, little enough time is allowed before this age for the natural maturing of their powers. This is what is meant by the oft-repeated warning that early specialisation is dangerous. Special training for a trade or profession, in spite of any clauses in Acts to the contrary, comes in theory and practice under the heading of technical

---

[1] The Parliamentary Return of June, 1898, gives the numbers as follows: Private Enterprise, 2886; Subscribers', 99; Companies', 99; Endowed, etc., 86; Local Authority, 3. It must again be mentioned that these figures include many schools which are not really secondary.

education; and to the same category belongs a woman's preparation for married life. But, unfortunately for the advocate of strict delimitation and organisation, the analogy does not hold beyond a certain point; for while a boy may be fairly expected to give distinct evidence of a decided aptitude for some special calling by the age of sixteen, every girl is a potential domestic economist.

Therefore to abandon totally the old aim of a girl's education is impossible; and there is a clearly marked reaction against the recent tendency to carry it on along the lines laid down for that of a boy. It must not be forgotten that, whether married or unmarried, woman possesses an influence in the world which is different in its character and action from that of a man. Social accomplishments are as necessary as ever to woman, if her influence is still to make for refinement and moral purity in England; but their attainment is no longer the only end of her education, as in earlier generations. Indeed, among the schoolmistresses of to-day, the great inclusive aim of all education—the complete harmonious realisation of normal capacities—is better understood than among men. It is certainly owing to their appreciation of this fundamental truth that women have become the pioneers in pedagogical research.

As might consequently be expected, it is chiefly on the intellectual side that the change in women's education is to be noticed. In spite of the refusal to admit them to the parliamentary franchise, or to recognise their claim to the degrees of our older

Universities, the intellectual force of women has made itself felt in public affairs and in every profession and path of life. An element has thus been introduced into national life which may be said to have been unknown to earlier generations. The so-called women's movement is both a cause and in its later aspects an effect of this development of the intellectual training of girls.

It may be safely averred that nowhere in the field of English education have such changes and reforms taken place within the last thirty years as in secondary schools for girls, and most important among these is the increased attention which is paid to intellectual studies.

In one respect has the tendency to carry on a girl's education along the lines which tradition has laid down for that of a boy led to unquestionably good results. I refer to the prominent place allotted to healthy physical exercise and English sports in the curriculum of every secondary girls' school that is not cut off from modern influences. It is impossible to overrate the skill and wisdom with which Englishwomen have introduced this new element into girls' education, and one cannot help comparing the success of their efforts with the failure of the attempt a few years ago to introduce our sports into the boys' schools of France.

The reform of secondary education for girls in this country is almost entirely the work of women, and, in contrast to some other countries, it is peculiarly significant that the recognised authorities on the education of women are women themselves. So fully is this admitted, that the Bryce Commission on Secondary Education included three women among its members, "the first of their sex ever appointed Royal Commissioners."[1]

It is a natural consequence that the schoolmistress is held in far higher estimation by the public than heretofore. The private governess also, who was formerly regarded as little better than a domestic servant, is now rapidly rising to the rank of an educational expert. To the teachers and head mistresses of the best secondary schools, who are among the foremost leaders of educational progress, is in a very large degree due the increased interest in educational questions which parents have evinced in recent years.

It is certain that men and women may be of mutual service in solving many of the purely educational problems which confront the Board of Education. In fact, with the probable spread of a modified form of co-education their co-operation would become essential.

Of the girls' schools, included in the Parliamentary Return of Secondary Schools, 91 per cent., as has already been stated, were private schools. There is nothing surprising in these figures. When it is remembered that social accomplishments are desired as much as ever for their daughters by those parents who can afford to give them a secondary education, it will be easily understood that class distinctions play a very large part in the division of girls' schools.

[1] GRAHAM BALFOUR, *The Educational Systems of Great Britain and Ireland*, p. 164. (Clarendon Press, 1898.)

Only private enterprise can meet the demand for variety thus created. Public day schools have done much to raise the standard of women's education, and there is little doubt that they have a great future before them. But, so long as class prejudices exist, it is hopeless to expect parents to consider educational efficiency before all else when selecting a school for their daughters. If to this is added all that has been said in favour of private schools for boys, an unanswerable case is made out for the continuation of the girls' private school.

At the same time, it would be foolish to close one's eyes to the fact that girls suffer as much as their brothers from all the defects invariably attaching to unbridled private enterprise in education. Fraud and imposture exist also among private schools for girls, and must be stamped out by the Board of Education. In their case there is, perhaps, even greater reason for suspecting that many so-called secondary schools provide education of a grade far inferior to what they pretend.

Wanted, a Census and Criterion of Efficiency.

The statistics furnished by the Parliamentary Return of Secondary Schools, to which I have more than once referred, are by far the most complete and reliable which exist. In fact, this Return is one of those revelations which make us feel that our Government offices do not altogether deserve the hard things that are said of them. They show at any rate that the Education Department is

NATIONAL RESOURCES

rapidly acquiring information as to the supply of secondary education in England; the method of arrangement adopted, so that certain defects stand out clearly before the eyes, gives evidence of an enlightened appreciation within the department of our educational needs.

But yet we may search in vain among these statistics for an answer to two questions of supreme importance. How many of these schools are really secondary? How many are efficient? So long as these two questions remain unanswered, the Board of Education has no firm foundation on which to build the work of organisation. This answer, then, will have to be found by the Board itself.

In the introductory memorandum to the Return it is observed that the information required for this purpose can only be obtained by means of inspection. I shall have a further opportunity of discussing the benefits of inspection; here it is only necessary to remark that no complete census can be taken of secondary schools until the range of secondary education has been determined, until a criterion of efficiency has been established, and inspectors appointed to visit all the schools in the country which claim to be secondary, in order to decide how far they come within this range and how closely they conform to the required standard of efficiency.

It would be a grave injustice to existing schools, and an unpardonable waste of public money, if the Board were to found, or to allow to be founded, new schools without having made every possible use of the actual supply. To inquire into this supply, to learn how far it meets, or is capable of being improved so as to meet, the material need must be the first step in reform. If this, and nothing else, were done thoroughly before the close of the century, the secondary department of the Board would at least have justified its creation.

But if some of the more prominent defects in the system, which have been touched on in the foregoing pages, are to be removed before they become deeply rooted; if, above all, the traditions of English secondary education are to be saved from extinction in our local endowed schools, this department of the Board will have to complete, with the least possible delay, the good work initiated by the Parliamentary Return, and proceed to the task of organisation for which it has been appointed.

CHAPTER III.

HIGHER TECHNICAL EDUCATION

I RECENTLY had the good fortune to visit one of those superb technical schools which testify to the determination of some of our large towns to supply our educational wants regardless of expense. On this particular school £15,000 of public money is spent yearly. I was naturally interested in its connection with the other local educational institutions, and on inquiring whether a boy who had passed through the highest class of the neighbouring grammar school would be admitted to the technical school without examination, I was informed that he would be too old for admission on any condition, and that, furthermore, he could only obtain technical instruction (if engineering be excepted) in the evening classes of that institution. It may be inferred, therefore, that in one of the foremost industrial centres of England, technical education is not considered of sufficient importance, for a boy who has received the best secondary education, to induce the public to provide him with the opportunities of devoting the whole of his energies for a longer or shorter period to technical studies.

The same town recently sent a committee to

inquire into and report on the provision for technical education in Germany. The committee returned with the information that its visit had been of little value, as the Germans began their technical education at the age at which English boys finished theirs. Now, here we have cause for serious reflection. That it would be folly to adopt foreign methods or systems of education, that Englishmen must solve their own problems for themselves if the result is to meet English needs and conditions of life, is no longer questioned by anyone who has given thought to these matters. But at the same time, the fact cannot be ignored that the popular demand for technical education was aroused by the great benefits accruing to the industries of Germany through her action in this special field; and the English people started out some years ago with the intention—in which they have persisted with marked consistency—of establishing a system at least as good, if not similar, in England. And yet we find that it comes as a surprise to the Technical Instruction Committee of one of our leading County Borough Councils to discover that the system they have established differs in its very foundations from that which is universal in Germany.

Before discussing the rival principles involved, it may be pointed out that there are exceptions to the system which I have taken as typical of England. The Science and Art Department, which directed the establishment of the technical school in the town in question, has no control over the secondary schools in the same locality, as they possess sufficient endowments to enable them to dispense with its financial aid. In another hardly less important town further north, the almost simultaneous action of the Science and Art Department was significantly different. There the grammar school had come under the control of this department in the manner explained in a former chapter. The technical college in this town was originally divided into two parts—one for higher and the other, resembling the school just alluded to, for lower technical education. With the consent of the Science and Art Department, however, the Technical Instruction Committee of this more fortunate city has abolished this lower school and bestowed a large share of its grants on the grammar school.

Now, the apparent inconsistency of the Science and Art Department in these two cases can only be excused on one ground. The science teaching in the grammar school cited in the first case was, as I have mentioned, not under the direction of this department, as in the latter; so that the Science and Art Department may have considered that, as representing the State, it should take every opportunity of bringing the science teaching, preparatory to technical education proper, under its control. But even then its justification is not fully established; for it may be objected, with some reason, that it is of more importance to establish technical schools, in which special training for various trades and industries may be given to boys who have had a good general education, than to create so-called technical schools in the sphere of secondary education. If we look back at the action of the Science and Art Department in connection with local endowed schools, in the light of this inconsistency, and it is only one of many examples, we must admit that this central authority has certainly lost few opportunities of extending its own powers. Can it be that, in view of the approaching reorganisation and delimitation of the spheres of the central educational authorities, it has done so in much the same spirit as has characterised certain European Powers in the unclaimed regions of Central Africa? No one but an advocate of the most extreme utilitarianism in education, if such a person now exist, can pretend that its action has been prompted by a patriotic consideration of the interests of the nation.

But to revert to the great technical high schools of Prussia, which first spurred us on by their example to expend money and energy on technical education. The particular point which should be noticed in connection with what has gone before is that no boy is admitted to these schools who has not obtained the "leaving certificate" of a secondary school; that is to say, who has not passed an examination, conducted by the masters of his school under the supervision of an inspector, in the whole range of subjects taught in the highest classes. The Prussian secondary schools are of three types (their curricula are published for all parents to see[1]): that in which Latin and Greek form the centre of studies, that in which Greek is replaced by a modern language, and that in which both

[1] An admirable translation of these has been made by Mr. W. G. Lipscomb, and appears in vol. iii. of *Special Reports on Educational Subjects*. (Eyre and Spottiswoode, 1898.)

Latin and Greek are omitted and modern languages, including the mother tongue, occupy the largest share of the pupils' attention. Boys obtain this leaving certificate at the age of eighteen or nineteen. The following opinion, emanating from Germany, may not be favourably received by our educational Chauvins; nevertheless, there is a firm conviction, among the teachers themselves in these technical schools, that their best pupils come from the fully classical secondary school—the first of the above divisions. Whether this be true or not—and I cannot help feeling that, if it is so, it points to a defect in the methods of teaching modern languages—the fact remains that the literary element predominates in all three types of German secondary schools, and that there is no attempt made within them to provide special training for any occupation, their sole object being to bestow a thorough general education.

There would be no need to consider here the foundations of Prussian technical education, had not the British public been persistently misinformed on this question by their popular educational leaders. Hence the astonishment of the various deputations sent by us to Germany when they discovered the truth. I repeat once more that it would be folly to transplant any foreign system into this country, but it is surely greater folly to adopt a misrepresentation of a foreign system. It is likewise folly, on the other hand, to attempt, from motives of mistaken patriotism, to make our system as dissimilar as possible from the foreign system. The foreigner's criticism of our educational system affects us little, but either of these three courses of action must render us ridiculous in his eyes.

The public has demanded, and rightly demanded, technical education for its children. By technical education they originally meant one thing only: "that those who are engaged in industry should have a trained intelligence and understanding of the special industries which they enter as bread-winners."[1] How is this to be obtained? We have just seen the German method. What has been the English one in the past? Whilst writing these pages a daily paper has been put into my hands containing an interesting passage on this question. Speaking of the author of a recent work on education, it says:—

"He is, however, quite out of harmony with feeling and opinion in the commercial world, when he contends that 'England has become strong in industry, exactly because she has never consciously set up the commercial or industrial standard in education, by educating her sons through specific curriculum for commerce and industry.' England is now doing the very thing Mr. Barnett flouts in this exaggerated statement of a partial truth. She is educating her sons for commerce and industry because they are in danger of falling behind in the great industrial race which the nations are running. It is true that education is one thing and instruction is another, but it is most important to the great world of commerce and industry that the unready Saxon should be trained to alertness, readiness, and promptitude, while he is taught the scientific basis on which industrial enterprise must rest."[2]

[1] PLAYFAIR, *Subjects of Social Welfare*, part iii. p. 307. (Cassell, 1889.)

[2] Extract from a review of Mr. P. A. BARNETT's *Common Sense in Education*. (Longmans and Co., 1899.)

Taking these words as a passage by themselves, without discussing the main principles of the book they refer to, we have an admirable illustration of the confusion of present-day educational thought in England. That "alertness, readiness, and promptitude" may be acquired without a "specific curriculum for commerce and industry" is so evident that it hardly needs emphasis. These three qualities are no more the natural inheritance of the German than of the Englishman, and yet they are possessed in no small measure by the boys who have passed through the German secondary schools. They are the results of *methods* of teaching and not of the subjects taught. But when we come to "the scientific basis on which industrial enterprise must rest" we reach the very kernel of our educational problem. Mr. Barnett is perfectly right, if we neglect other outside causes, in claiming that our past phenomenal success in industry and commerce has been due in a very large degree to the choice by our secondary schools of a range of subjects well adapted to the formation of character, and not necessarily directly connected with a boy's future occupation.

At the same time, it must be admitted that the advance of civilisation has raised many branches of commerce and industry to a science, demanding a special training for its practice just as Medicine, Law, or Education. But does the doctor or lawyer begin the special studies connected with his science at the age of twelve or thirteen? And yet we have never considered our doctors or lawyers as second to any in the world. The analogy is perfectly sound—

unless all the talk about commercial and industrial science is nonsense—and we must face the fact that we cannot treat commerce and industry as if they were not amenable to the same educational laws as other sciences. If there is any truth in the principle that the technical education of the man of commerce and industry must begin at the age of twelve, then the principle likewise applies to men destined for other occupations of the same scientific rank, and we must be prepared to found special secondary schools for most trades and professions.

In former days England, just as Germany does to-day, based all special training on, as far as possible, a broad, common foundation. Any other system is illogical, opposed to every sound tradition, and, if carried out consistently, economically impossible.

The need for technical education in commerce and industry has, however, become very pressing. The country is well provided with medical schools, second to none in the world. How many commercial or industrial schools have we of similar rank? And yet it was to encourage and create them that the Science and Art Department was founded. We shall look to the Board of Education to repair this defect, and to afford every facility for the study of the scientific bases on which commercial and industrial enterprise must rest, while at the same time increasing the supply and efficiency of our secondary education—that foundation on which future generations will depend for their moral force and character. At the present moment we can afford less than ever to forget that the best secondary education will do more than any legislation to prevent the spread of corruption among our commercial classes, and to preserve them worthy of the great English traditions of the past.

NOTE.—There exists a good deal of confusion in the use of the term "technical education." To the popular imagination it conveys the idea of special industrial training only; for the student of the English language it connotes all special training for any occupation. The latter is probably the meaning which it will ultimately adopt. Confusion has been made worse confounded by the action of the Science and Art Department. In sanctioning the application of various moneys to the encouragement of this branch of education, Parliament has delegated to the department the interpretation of this term. In its attempts, related in the preceding pages, to extend its control, the Science and Art Department has expanded its interpretation of this term until it includes the teaching of almost every subject save Latin and Greek. Consequently, some people have wished to use the word "technological" to represent, as it literally does, the popular meaning of "technical." But, if only for the reason that it is unwise to impose new terms on the public, particularly in the case of a subject in which it is so deeply interested, this innovation is hardly to be recommended. It would be far better to rescue the word "technical" from the private possession of the Science and Art Department, restore it to its original meaning, and lead the people to see that technical education includes special training for any occupation.

CHAPTER IV.

AGRICULTURAL EDUCATION

IT is difficult to say whether our education is exposed to greater dangers from the absurd desire of some persons to transplant foreign methods and systems into this country, or from that false patriotism which refuses to admit that the foreigner can teach us anything. The latter has, however, become alarmingly widespread in recent years. In matters educational, more than one great thinker, proud of the achievements of England, and persuaded of the incomparable strength of the English character, has been branded as unpatriotic because he has attempted to point a moral from the educational progress of foreign nations. That the disciples of these men have in no way departed from the work which they initiated, is an additional proof of the stubborn persistency of Englishmen in the support of right when they have once clearly seen it. In a report, for example, on " Recent Educational Progress in Denmark,"[1] Mr. J. S. Thornton draws attention to the fact that the present agricultural prosperity of the Danes is to be traced to what

---

[1] *Special Reports on Educational Subjects*, vol. i. (Eyre and Spottiswoode.)

may appear a mere detail to many persons, but what is, nevertheless, one of the fundamental truths of education—a truth which has been unceasingly preached in this country by all writers speaking with authority. He tells us that, in an address which excited a good deal of comment at the Oxford Summer Meeting of 1894, Mr. Alfred Poulsen, President of the Association of Danish High Schools, said, in connection with the question of Danish butter: "The greater part of the men and women who manufacture this butter are pupils of the high schools."

On these People's high schools the State has since 1892 spent over £16,000 yearly. They consist of "sixty-five adult boarding schools or residential colleges, attended by students of the peasant or yeoman class for the most part, the greater number between the ages of eighteen and twenty-five, though many are still older." At most of them the men attend in the winter and the women in the summer. "There are besides these sixty-five people's high schools, five agricultural and two horticultural schools on similar lines, as well as seven schools which are partly high schools and partly agricultural schools. At these seventy-nine schools there must be over six thousand men and women from humble homes receiving instruction every year. . . . At the agricultural schools the better half of the students, those who seize most completely and apply most readily what they learn there, have first been students of history and literature in the ordinary high school."

From this short description a general idea of the

system may be gathered, but it is the spirit which underlies or is rather the motive power of this system which accounts for its success.

It is interesting to notice, as a further proof of what we have taught the foreigner, that this spirit was inspired by the England of 1830. Bishop Grundtvig, who started the idea of these schools, felt, when visiting England about this date in the pursuance of literary studies, that something more than books was needed to give the Danes that energy and activity which he noted among our fathers. To the superficial observer there may not seem to be a very close connection between the educational principles which he laid down and the successful manufacture of butter! But it is a connection which we should do well to appreciate. Among the teachers in the high schools, he says, there ought to be at least one who is "a master of the mother tongue, not only as it is found in books, but as it lives in the nation . . . at least one who knows and loves our Fatherland's history, and is able to picture it vividly in words . . . at least one who knows and loves our national songs . . . at least one who has seen much of our Fatherland . . . and one who could give the youth a true and living apprehension of our Fatherland's constitution and laws formerly and now."

The staff of masters here proposed would have created national schools in the truest sense. The attitude of the Church towards education in Denmark is instructive: a bishop initiated this movement, and theological students have continued it to a successful issue.

The chief feature of the teaching in these schools appears to be lessons which take the form of conversations. Thus we find conversations of an hour's duration in physics two days a week, universal history two days, history of the North three days, and Bible lesson one day. The other subjects taught in a typical high school are historical geometry (to be carefully distinguished from the succession of *pontes asinorum* which are the terror of our schoolmasters), statistics, gymnastics, singing, Danish, English, geography, book-keeping, and arithmetic. The expenses of a student for six months at any of these schools will be covered by £12 or £13, including apparently every possible need (even tobacco) with the exception of dress. But in spite of the lowness of these fees "the poorer half of the students readily obtain through the County Council a bursary that covers one half their expenses."

It will thus be seen that the Danes distinguish between education and instruction, and believe that the latter is worthless without the former. It may appear a paradox to the uninitiated, but instruction in the principles of butter-making is by no means the first requirement for the promotion of the butter industry. But yet that is the principle which we have applied to industrial or commercial education in England. The Science and Art Department, as we have seen, is always ready to bestow grants for the encouragement of the teaching of special subjects to boys and girls as soon as they have left the elementary schools. The Danes have grasped the fact that even dairy and egg farming need before everything else intelligence, and the whole of their educational machinery is directed to the training of that intelligence, and to the fostering of a healthy patriotism—one of the greatest incentives to a desire for the highest possible self-realisation.

It is certain that no real revival of agriculture will take place in England until we lay greater stress in our rural schools on the training of the intelligence. But while the present popular tendency to regard the accumulation of knowledge as the first object of education must be strenuously opposed, it would be equally fatal to the interests of teaching to consider the training of the intelligence as the sole, or even the most important, function of our schools. It is possible, however, now that we have a Consultative Committee of experts, that the consideration of the peculiar conditions affecting the decline of agriculture may lead our departments to a higher appreciation of the aims of education, and to a fuller recognition of the principles governing the physical, mental, and moral development of man than have characterised our Codes and Directories of the past.

Of the forces which militate against the revival of English agriculture, those do not concern us here which legislation might or might not eradicate without impairing the strength of the whole nation. But there is one which education might do much to counteract, and that is the attraction of town life for a large section of the rural population. This attraction to each individual varies directly in strength as his ignorance of the economic conditions which govern national progress—an ignorance which is often accompanied by moral weakness which is powerless against the allurements of the streets of our large towns. Now, while the very nature of our constitution makes it impossible that education should be regarded, as in some other lands, as a legitimate instrument for moulding the minds of the people to the views of the governing classes, the enlightenment of ignorance and the imparting of moral strength are two of its highest functions.

To earn a living is the primary object of most workers, but man does not live by bread alone; and while it is undoubtedly one of the duties of education to prepare men for bread-winning, it has also the higher duty of inspiring them with the power of obtaining the greatest moral benefit from the performance of their work. A worker of trained intelligence may prove a satisfactory producer of wealth; but it is the man who loves his work, and regards it as a means for realising all that is best in himself, who is the highest type of citizen. It will therefore fare ill with the nation if, in reforming its education, it does no more than substitute, as a preparation for technical instruction, the training of the intelligence for the accumulating of knowledge. It is extraordinary how apt people are to forget, in discussing educational problems, that, if good workers are to be produced, it is necessary first of all to foster some propelling force which will urge them to overcome the inevitable obstacles in life. There is a famous school of German philosophers who claim that the main object of instruction is the arousing of interest. Though this may be only a partial truth, yet interest is certainly a propelling force, if not the source of all forces of the kind; and if the result of our education were only to arouse a keen interest in the pupil's future surroundings it would indeed have accomplished much. The agriculturist's love of his work, for instance, must depend on his interest in Nature. It should be easy enough to arouse such an interest in rural schools; and interest in Nature, leading to the discovery of the benefits of living in close contact with Nature, would not only make a better worker of the agriculturist, but would strengthen him morally against, at any rate the lower, attractions of town life.

Such an interest would be best aroused by the teaching of science in the elementary school, not by reference to coloured plates and printed formulæ, but from the great object-lessons going on in the fields around; not that science which fills narrow minds to the exclusion of literature, but that which is illuminated by the poet's fancy and wooed by the imagination. A country child should know something about the weeds and flowers of surrounding field and wayside, the names and habits of common birds and beasts, something of insect pests for use, and something of moths and butterflies for pleasure, something of the life of ponds and rivers, as much as is clear and simple of the processes of Nature.

The agriculturist, unlike the artisan, will never separate Nature and science in earning his daily bread. The artisan in our towns uses the forces of Nature without necessarily coming into direct contact with the great generatrix. These forces have been wrested by science from Nature, stored by man in machinery of his own invention, and placed at the disposal of the workman in a form from which all the æsthetic and moral influences of Nature's inspiration have been eliminated. Rarely is he reminded in his daily work that man is dependent on Nature; if he ever thinks of her it is rather as a handmaiden obedient to his beck and call to minister to wants of his own creation, and to assist in her own effacement. With the agriculturist it is quite otherwise. He lives in direct contact with her, and he is dependent on her for the success of his bread-winning. Science is of service to him only in so far as it enables him to aid her in overcoming the obstacles which stand in the way of the highest development of her own productiveness. Can it, then, be difficult to teach science to the young agricultural labourer in such a way that it will give him a lasting interest in Nature, and a love for his work which will form an adamantine chain against the tide which flows townwards?

But so far we have only considered the necessity of arousing interest in the immediate surroundings of daily life. There is also an outer circle of environment of no less importance—that which we may term national life. To educate a child as an isolated individual, or even as a member of a small community, would not satisfy modern requirements. He must be brought up to play his part as a member of the nation. His interest must be aroused in the economic laws which affect national progress. This may be best attained by the teaching of history; and even before leaving the elementary school he may have discovered some of the responsibilities of the agriculturist with regard to the maintenance of our national supremacy. An additional influence will thus be established against the attractions of town life. Interest in the welfare of the nation will engender a patriotism to give the highest motive to his daily work; and ignorance of the conditions of wage-earning in our cities will no longer lead him to desert his village, "to see profusion that he must not share."

But it is evident that the educational principles, of which a faint outline has been sketched, cannot be carried out without efficient teachers. This fact suggests the fundamental weakness of our system. Rural School Boards offer poor testimony to the virtues of democracy; and, speaking generally, the best work in country districts is done by voluntary schools. But, unfortunately, the funds at the disposal of the latter are so inadequate that the State cannot insist on the proper efficiency of the teachers they employ. Our first duty, nevertheless, is to provide the most highly trained teaching in our rural schools. If the country people are unwilling to help themselves, the State will either have to become responsible for the maintenance of existing voluntary schools, or found other institutions under more satisfactory control than that of the School Boards. It is to be hoped that the nation in its present prosperity will not shun the difficulties that confront it, and, above all, will not allow itself to be further deluded into the fatal compromise of offering technical instruction to half-educated children. The advance of a modern state in civilisation may at present be measured by the extent to which it has brought secondary education within the reach of all classes of the people.

The powers of the Board of Agriculture in matters relating to education are to be taken over by the Board of Education; so that this latter body will be able to bring agricultural education into its proper connection with the whole national system. The Board of Agriculture has so far confined its attention to supporting collegiate centres of agricultural education in England and Wales, and in aiding important agricultural experiments. The grants which it awarded to the institutions receiving assistance amounted in the year 1898-99 to £7350. None of this money can be spared for agricultural education of the grade which I have so far alluded to. Indeed, while higher agricultural education will naturally come under the control of the Technical Educational Department, the lower sections must be supervised by the Secondary and Elementary Departments. It is to them we must look for a wise solution of this difficult but pressing problem. At first it will doubtless be expedient to extend the Evening Continuation School system so as to provide lower technical education in agriculture for country boys and girls. To meet the need, proper attendance at such schools should, during the months when work is slackest, be made compulsory for all children as soon as they leave the elementary schools. It will certainly be many years before such

F

provision of education will be made in our rural districts that boys and girls of fourteen to sixteen may take advantage of it when their physical and mental powers are fresh and unwearied. But we must never forget that Evening Continuation Schools can only be regarded as a makeshift and temporary system.

CHAPTER V.

ORGANISATION OF THE BOARD OF EDUCATION

WE have seen that whatever false steps have been taken in the development of secondary and technical education during recent years are due, almost exclusively, to the imperfect organisation of the central educational authority. Secondary education, calling in vain for Government aid, has suffered grievously from the encroachment of technical education, which has been under the fostering care of a strong department with large funds directly or indirectly at its disposal. Technical education has thus grown rapidly, but has seriously weakened itself in attempts to extend its boundaries at the cost of that very ally on whom it depended for the source of all its vital force. It is scarcely necessary to remark that the two should have made common cause in working towards one national aim.

Fortunately we have not adopted the same methods of government in colonising abroad as in organising our education at home. It has never yet happened, for instance, that we have granted a company a royal charter, recognising its right to develop territory at its own expense, and then, having sent out an imperial expedition to develop neighbouring territory, allowed it to become utterly unmanageable and to devote imperial resources to an attack on the company, which had grown weak and enfeebled. But if we replace the company by the Charity Commissioners, and the imperial expedition by the Science and Art Department, we obtain a true picture of the struggle which has been waged over secondary and technical education in England.

The natural solution of the difficulty which would have arisen from this imaginary, but fortunately unrealisable, blunder in colonising, would have been for the Imperial Government to do away with the chartered company and, taking its most efficient officers into its service, form a new force to govern the disputed territory. Thus both colonies might be placed on the same footing under the control of the Colonial Office, and brought into their proper relation with other national efforts of the same kind.

Very similar means must be adopted to save us from our educational muddles, and it is for this purpose that the Board of Education has been created.

The organisation of our central government presenting such a want of system as to baffle the most cautious student, analogies between any two departments are often deceptive. The comparison already instituted between colonial and educational affairs may, however, be pursued with advantage in a somewhat different direction. When it was determined, in 1858, to vest in Her Majesty the territories then under the government of the East India Company, a new and distinct branch of the central government

THE BOARD OF EDUCATION 69

was created, to which were given, together with other powers, those formerly exercised by the Indian Board of Control. The conditions, which had characterised the development of India, had been so totally different from those affecting our other dependencies and colonies, that it would have been disastrous to place it under the control of the Colonial Office (or any other office doing colonial work).

For similar reasons, when it was determined to bring secondary education under the control of the State, the general consensus of opinion was in favour of placing it under a new office, distinct from those already created for the control of primary and technical education. To this office, it was thought, might be transferred, together with other powers, those formerly exercised by the Charity Commissioners, just as certain powers of the Commissioners of the Board of Control had been given to the new Indian branch of the central government. So different, indeed, are the conditions which have characterised the development of secondary education under the partial control of the Charity Commissioners, and those affecting the other two branches, controlled and to a very large extent founded by the State, that a new department is evidently required.

We have thus two precedents of colonial government to guide us in the organisation of the Board of Education. While secondary education may claim a distinct office for its control, with as much reason as India, it possesses as close an affinity of aim to the other branches of education as our imaginary colonies of the first illustration to one another. We must therefore combine these two precedents, and thus arrive at the logical organisation of the new education office which, we have been told, the Board of Education will adopt.

Under the President of the Board, who, saving the title, will be Minister of Education, must be three distinct departments, presided over by one permanent secretary, who thus represents the common aim. Their independence will be secured, and at the same time due observance of the common aim will be assured, by the appointment of an assistant secretary at the head of each, who is directly responsible to the permanent secretary for the management of his department. The organisation is remarkable in that it presents those clearly defined features and practical divisions, easily understood by the public, which are not conspicuous in our other Government offices.

The great responsibility which will fall on the shoulders of the permanent secretary is immediately evident. However enthuiastic may be his three assistant secretaries, there must at first be a certain amount of friction—a period of storm and stress must intervene between the chaos of the past and the harmonious organisation of the future. In short, the post of permanent secretary will be precisely one of that kind in which English public servants have so often distinguished themselves and been gratefully remembered by posterity—and occasionally failed and been forgotten.

The harmonious working of the three forces under his direction is the ultimate object to be kept before

THE BOARD OF EDUCATION 71

the eyes of the chief permanent secretary. Deep knowledge of our educational needs, and unwearying tact and sympathy, will be essential to its attainment; but harmony must not be established at the sacrifice of a single fraction of the power which must, in the interest of the nation, be maintained by each of these forces.

Of the three, the weakest for some time to come may, unless it is directed with extraordinary ability, be the Secondary Department. The Technical Department — the Science and Art Department reformed and rechristened—possesses great strength, but, as we have seen, its energy has been misdirected in the past. The Primary Department—that branch which is now popularly known as the Education Department—will be the force which, both in direction and power, will at first show itself most effective.

It may perhaps be wise to emphasise the fact once again, that the fundamental cause which led to the establishment of the Board of Education was the urgent need for organisation in secondary education; the wise appreciation on the part of Lord Salisbury's Government of the necessity of uniting the three departments in a national aim alone accounts for the presence of the two other factors in the problem. Now, it is only natural that the existing departments should regard the new Secondary Department with jealousy. It will consequently be the duty of the chief permanent secretary to shield it from all outside attacks during the early years of its growth and development. But to show any consideration for this jealousy when selecting the assistant secretary who is to preside over its early destinies would probably prove fatal to the very object for which it was created. The difficulties which it will have to face in its internal organisation, and in accustoming all the untamed secondary forces to its control, will tax to the utmost the tact and energy of the strongest man. If any jealousies or susceptibilities whatever are to be taken into account, they can only be those of the secondary schools themselves; it is certainly of importance that the first assistant secretary should command their fullest confidence.

Perhaps there is, however, no more hopeful sign for the success of this department than the present attitude of these schools towards reform. Even the head masters of the great public schools have shown themselves ready to take their proper place at the head of the great movement that is destined not only to organise our system of schools, but to further develop our methods of education so as to adapt them most perfectly to modern requirements. The keenest interest has been displayed by all schoolmasters in foreign educational methods, from which, as they recognise, they may learn many useful lessons; but, at the same time, they are convinced that the spread of the best influences of our great public schools, throughout the whole field of secondary education, is an indispensable condition of reform along national lines. We have seen how the local endowed schools have striven to remain under these influences, and how poverty alone deflected them from their natural line of development. The part played by the Science and Art Department in this work is faithfully reflected in the recent utterance of a member of one of the County Technical Instruction Committees, who has openly advocated the widening of the line of cleavage between the local and non-local (*i.e.* public) schools. But fortunately the assistant secretary to the new department will receive the support of an overwhelming majority of feeling in lifting local endowed schools on to the plane from which they have fallen, and establishing them there firmly, with sufficient resources to maintain their position. One is therefore almost guilty of uttering a platitude in saying that no efforts must be spared to induce the great public schools to come under the new department, thus to act as a great leavening power among all secondary schools, and in their turn to receive from humbler institutions much light and guidance in their attempts to solve the complex problems of modern secondary education.

Perhaps there is nothing that the secondary schools, and particularly the public schools, dread more than that the traditions of past departments should be brought to bear on their own development. The grounds for their dread of the Science and Art Department have already been explained at some length; the failure of the Charity Commission, for which its members are not alone to blame, to take full advantage of the powers bestowed on them by the Endowed Schools Act has not raised them very high in the public esteem, and the not altogether wise spirit which has occasionally characterised their manner of exercising their undoubted rights over educational forces has not endeared them to all secondary schools, and perhaps least of all to assistant masters.

But it is the tradition of what has been popularly known as the Education Department that all types of secondary schools unite in fearing. It should be remembered that the function of this department has been to administer the Elementary Education Acts of 1870 to 1897. Now, these Acts may be said to be the outcome of two distinct and, in a sense, mutually counteracting forces. First we may notice the growing conviction that each step towards democracy—that is to say, each lowering of the suffrage and admission of a number of illiterate persons to a share in the government of the nation—must be accompanied by a proportionate spread of education. To say that the English people as a whole have ever demanded education as one of the indefeasible and fundamental rights of man, "next to bread," as Danton said, is certainly an exaggeration. Were it true, we should have seen education preparing the way for, rather than following in the train of, the extension of the franchise; or at any rate it would never have been necessary to compel the lower class by penal enactments to send their children to school. We must rather regard the conviction of the necessity of universal elementary education among the educated classes themselves as the chief force which carried the Act of 1870; and among no section of the community was this stronger than among those who from sincerely patriotic, if mistaken, motives had opposed each extension of the franchise. The second force, however, and the one which delayed

THE BOARD OF EDUCATION

the spread of education more than any other, was the strife for religious freedom, more radically desirable in education than in aught else.

It is now an old story how it seemed impossible for Government to supply and control elementary education until a compromise, which satisfied the majority of religious denominations, was arrived at as to instruction in religion. The weary debates in Parliament not only resulted in banishing all religious doctrines, to which a majority of the sects did not subscribe, from the schools established under the Act of 1870, but also warned the department against the introduction of any contentious moral principle in the education under its control. But, as we have seen, the ethical side of education, based as it often is on honest difference of religious belief, is precisely the strongest feature in English secondary education. There is no doubt that the elimination of the higher ethical side of education from the elementary schools, which are wholly under the control of the State, has enormously simplified the administrative work of the Education Department. But for this very reason it has created an impression, deeply engraved on the official mind, that educational problems can be solved by the rule of red tape. Even the inspectors, who often bring to their work the best traditions of English education, are sooner or later compelled to abandon their ideals, and to build up a theory of education, hedged in by official restrictions and dealing only with intellectual development, training in mental agility, and the acquisition of knowledge; as if these in themselves comprised the whole aim of education. And if even the inspectors have been obliged to subscribe to such a theory, what must have been the effect on teachers?

Such are the traditions to which secondary schools of every type are determined not to submit, and public opinion will support them in that determination. It was the fear lest these traditions should have any influence in the new Secondary Department which raised the irresistible demand for a Consultative Committee that might be able to combat them. The functions of this committee will be dealt with in a later chapter; here it must suffice to notice that, through it, the profession and the public will be able to bring considerable pressure to bear on the assistant secretary for secondary education should it be necessary.

But it must not be imagined that mere passivity of the administrative hand is all that is needed. From what has been already said, it is evident that active intervention will be necessary to save the local endowed schools from degradation or extinction. To save them from extinction much administrative talent will have to be brought into play; to save them from degradation a deep appreciation of and sympathy with their highest aim, that of preparing for the Universities, will be necessary. The Board of Education will not be empowered to exercise any direct control over the Universities, but a competent head of the Secondary Department, in whom the Universities have confidence, will be able to do much to remove any obstacles which they may in the past have

THE BOARD OF EDUCATION 77

placed in the way of the modern development of secondary education; they may even be persuaded to restore many of their scholarships to their original purpose—the provision of the highest education, free of cost, for poor students—and thus place us, in this respect, on a level with other less democratic nations.

Above all, in order that harmony may gradually grow up among the three departments, it will be necessary for the chief permanent secretary continually to meet his three assistant secretaries in conference, to guide them towards the common national aim and to restrain all inclination to encroach on one another's territories. Competition may be a great stimulus to high achievement, but rivalry of aim has not so far promoted the best interests of education. Emulation between schools of a similar type may be desirable; so may emulation between the whole educational system of different localities. But rivalry between department and department, or between schools with distinct aims, can only result in overlapping and waste of public funds and energy.

Neither should the influence which the Secondary Department may exercise on the other two offices be forgotten. In administrative experience it will probably remain inferior to the other departments for some years to come. This will not, however, necessarily be a disadvantage. But if it be provided with the best possible *personnel* it may do much, by its mere influence, to assist the Primary Department to raise the tone of the education in our elementary schools, and thus save us from the moral degeneration of those countries which have based the education of the great mass of the voters solely on an intellectual theory; and it may promote a cause of hardly less value to the nation in aiding the Technical Department to provide that higher technical and commercial education which hitherto has been so grievously neglected in England.

CHAPTER VI.

THE CONSULTATIVE COMMITTEE

IN the last chapter reference was made to certain aspects of colonial government. To go into no new regions for precedents, some others of these aspects may now be considered. The impossibility of obtaining accurate knowledge as to the needs of colonies far distant from our shores has induced the home authorities to bestow on some of them a large measure of self-government, for thus alone can conditions familiar only to men on the spot be satisfied. In the case of India, however, self-government is as yet an impossibility, and this great dependency is therefore controlled by the Imperial Government acting through a Secretary of State advised by a council of experts. Certain broad conclusions as to the control of education may be drawn from the precedents thus established. That of separate offices for each branch of education has already been noted. That of local self-government will be dealt with in another chapter; and we need not go outside the mother country for precedents in its favour. For the present purpose some of the peculiar difficulties which led to the establishment of the Council of India need alone be noticed.

The highest conception of the government of a dependency is the ruling of the inhabitants for their own good. That of India, with its vast, heterogeneous population, presents many problems outside the ken of the British public and the great majority of members of Parliament. The Oriental mind is so utterly different from the European mind that no Englishman, who has not studied and observed its workings for years, can possibly understand its peculiarities. Neither can the social and economic conditions affecting Indian life be understood without long experience in their midst. To attempt to govern India by the administrative methods which have been adopted in the past for home affairs would be disastrous. On the other hand, the national honour being deeply implicated in the success of this government, opportunity must be given for the expression and influence of the national conscience on the various broad issues which may arise; for, as Sir Charles Dilke remarks in this connection, "in these days no institution not supported by the constituencies at home can long survive."[1]

So that, while Parliament is fully justified in watching over the action of the government of India, the principle at any rate is excellent that a council, consisting of men who have gained practical experience in Indian affairs, should advise the Secretary of State, and, through him, supply Parliament with expert counsel on the various problems which may arise. Many of the arguments which may

[1] *Problems of Greater Britain*, p. 394.

be advanced in favour of the existence of this council of experts for India apply with even greater force to the establishment of a similar council in connection with the State control of education in England.

In secondary education, in particular, we have a heterogeneous system of schools, in the sense that, apart from the common aim which must be possessed by all, there are many different types supplying various needs. The distinctions between them are often so subtle that they do not appeal to the practical statesman, who is obliged to take a telescopic rather than a microscopic view of the various forces in national life; but yet they constitute one of the main principles on which the delicate machinery of English education is founded. They, together with the means by which they are ensured and the effects which they produce, can only be understood by those who have studied and observed their workings for years. To attempt to control national education by the administrative methods which have been adopted in the past for other national forces would surely, sooner or later, lead to disaster.

The apparent failure of the Council of India to command the confidence of Parliament—the eminent authority whom I have already quoted, states that when "any members of the House of Commons who have given some attention to Indian affairs bring forward resolutions, the opinion of the Council, even if unanimous, weighs not one feather's weight in the balance"[1]—cannot be accepted as a final condemna-

[1] *Problems of Greater Britain*, p. 407.

tion of the system itself. Mr. Lecky would account for this failure by the fact that "when a small group of voters may turn the balance, the great interests of India are too likely to be sacrificed to the party game."[1]

But this is not so likely to be the case with regard to the Consultative Committee which is to advise the President of the Board of Education on all questions referred to it. It is well known that educational debates are of all the most unpopular in Parliament, and, even should their popularity revive, any party would hesitate to ignore the opinion of the Board when supported by the Consultative Committee; for the immediate effects of any blunder would be much more conspicuous in matters concerning education at home than in affairs connected with a far distant dependency. Not that Parliament will renounce one jot of its rights to safeguard the liberties of the people, which may be so easily and insidiously undermined when once the control of education is vested in the State.

Not only does the control of education present difficulties at least as great as the government of a vast heterogeneous population, moved by impulses strange to the European mind, but education is one of the most complex forces in modern civilisation, and, as I have already suggested, its vitality depends on the teachers' freedom of initiative. Here therefore the analogy, which I have drawn between the two systems of government, ceases. "The Indian governmental system is too regular," again to quote

[1] *Democracy and Liberty*, p. 208.

Sir Charles Dilke, "the codes are too complete, traditions too strong, to give much room to human personality."[1]

This is doubtless right and necessary for the government of India; but although personality is, if not everything, the greatest factor in education, the same words might well be applied to the past control of elementary education. As we have seen, that is precisely why the secondary schools dread the influence of the old Education Department. While therefore Parliament may be concerned in protecting the liberty of the people, the Consultative Committee must stand as the champion of the liberty of teachers. Not its least important function will consequently be to withstand any attempts of Parliament or the Board to fetter the personality of the secondary teacher and to hedge him in with too many restrictions; it may even succeed, in the not far distant future, in removing some of those cast-iron rules and regulations which have been imposed on the elementary teacher.

But, at the same time, the Consultative Committee must actively help in the work of organisation. Its two most important duties will be to form a register of teachers and to aid in the selection of a body of capable inspectors. How registration and inspection are the indispensable foundations of all organisation, and what part the Consultative Committee must play in promoting each, will be shown in succeeding chapters. There is one important function of this committee, however, which has been overlooked in many quarters, and demands especial notice here.

[1] *Problems of Greater Britain*, p. 435.

The average status of assistant masters in secondary schools is certainly lower in England than in any other European country. That they are too often, in fact with the exception of those in the great public schools one might say always, inadequately paid is known to all who have inquired into the matter. But this is an evil which, unfortunately, can only be remedied gradually and with some consideration of the law of supply and demand. That they should also, in many instances, be handicapped in their work by the ever-present fear of capricious dismissal is, however, a wrong which the nation, in its own interests, should take the first opportunity of redressing. Cases of peculiar hardship in this respect have recently come before the public, and perhaps the sacrifice of several men, who had for years given satisfaction to their employers, could not have occurred at a more opportune moment; for the country has now the opportunity of providing security of tenure for all assistant masters.

These members of the teaching profession have put forward the plea, persistently for the last twenty-five years, that they should be allowed a right of appeal against dismissal to some responsible and unprejudiced body. In this they have been supported by many head masters, who are anxious to remove a stumbling-block from the path of some of their weaker and less enlightened brethren, and to maintain a high standard of dignity within their ranks. In some instances a right of appeal to the governing body of a school has been allowed, but has occasionally led to a regrettable display of local

CONSULTATIVE COMMITTEE 85

prejudices and ill feeling. It is far better that, should any case of unjust dismissal unfortunately occur, it should be dealt with by the Board of Education, acting through the Consultative Committee as representing the highest expert knowledge on matters educational in this country.

Looked at in its wider aspects, the consent of Parliament to the creation of such a Consultative Committee, in connection with a department of the home government, has a deep and far-reaching significance. It amounts to a recognition of the dangers, perceived for many years by keen observers of the trend of national events, arising from the struggle between democracy and bureaucracy. However admirable may be the Acts passed by Parliament, their effect depends entirely on the manner in which they are administered. To say nothing of the influence which departments may exercise on the framing of a measure, they are necessarily allowed very considerable freedom in carrying out its provisions. The selection of Civil Servants by means of competitive examinations has no doubt raised the *personnel* of our Government offices to a standard never before attained. But such examinations prove only the intellectual ability of the young men and women who enter the Civil Service; their knowledge of the special branch of national life with which they have to deal is acquired only from the point of view of outside control necessarily adopted by the office in which they serve. Further knowledge is needed both for the guidance of Parliament and the departments. Such can only be obtained by collecting the opinion of those who have distinguished themselves most highly in the various branches themselves. Having now been applied to the control of education, and in a modified form to some other departments of government, this principle will certainly extend to those other branches of the Civil Service where it is as yet unknown, and ultimately will put an end to that government by ignorance which has too often characterised bureaucracy in the past.

But the idea must not for a moment be entertained that either Parliament or the departments will consent to be advised by a pedantocracy; and herein lies a danger which it will require peculiar care, in establishing the Consultative Committee, to avoid. Pedants it must not contain, neither faddists, but men and women who have had practical experience in educating, and who have distinguished themselves in the teaching profession, as well as those who represent education in its relation to the varied demands of national life. At one time, when it was intended that this committee should deal only with the question of the registration of teachers, it was thought that no less than two-thirds of its members should be directly elected by different groups of teachers, whose interests would be involved in the formation of a register. But, now that it will be allotted a wider sphere of responsibility, it is evident that the directly elected representatives of special interests, not necessarily or even probably the best exponents of educational thought, can have no place among its members.

At the same time, it is a wise provision that it should consist, "as to not less than two-thirds, of persons *qualified to represent the views* of universities and other bodies interested in education." The selection of all its members will practically rest with the President of the Board, and, while it is evident from what has gone before that the head masters of the public and local endowed schools and the head mistresses of girls' schools must certainly be among them, it will be of the greatest value to the Board to obtain through the Consultative Committee the opinion of assistant teachers on many points connected with the organisation of secondary education. One of these points, that which may be said to lie at the root of all reform, has been dealt with in this chapter.

The Consultative Committee must represent the highest expert opinion in the land. It must not on this account be deaf to the less experienced advocates of many pressing reforms of detail in our system of schools. But, above all, it should contain at least one member (the committee must necessarily be a small one) who will bring to its deliberations a profound knowledge of the variety of local needs; so that it may be consulted with profit on the very difficult problems, which the Board must immediately face, in connection with the creation of local authorities. That the first essential condition to the usefulness of the Consultative Committee is sympathy with the assistant secretary to the Secondary Department may be repeated, for it is a fact on which it is impossible to insist too strongly.

CHAPTER VII.

THE REGISTRATION OF TEACHERS

THE relation of the teacher to his profession may be likened to that of the soldier to his regiment—with this important difference, that the position of the teacher is a more isolated one, and that the successful performance of his duties depends to a greater extent on his individual fitness and energy. It is therefore evident, allowing, which none will deny, that the art of education is at least as valuable to the nation as that of war, that even more attention should be paid to the qualifications of our teachers than to those of our soldiers. And yet, while enormous sums of money are spent on the drilling of the latter, and while public opinion has insisted during recent years on the attainment of a higher standard of efficiency in our army, the training of secondary teachers is popularly considered as no object of national concern. In this respect we stand alone among civilised nations.

Or to draw another comparison. Few parents would, for the sake of economy, entrust the bodies of their children to the hands of a doctor who was not a fully qualified practitioner; and yet, when it is a question of selecting educators for the mental and moral development of their children, many will

REGISTRATION OF TEACHERS 89

not hesitate to act, or connive at action, on the principle of buying in the cheapest market. The results of the application of this principle have been most disastrous where competition has been freest, that is to say, in private schools; for in them, according to the statistics furnished by the Parliamentary Return so frequently alluded to in these pages, more than half of the men and about seven-eighths of the women teachers have not passed the degree examinations of a British University. Now, whatever this may prove, one conclusion may be confidently drawn, namely, that the British public has allowed by far the greater number of secondary schoolmasters and schoolmistresses to teach its children without having satisfied the only recognised test of efficiency. That it is the only recognised test of efficiency is proved by the fact that the public has offered, as its excuse for its indifference to the question of the training of secondary teachers, the conviction that the possession of a university degree is a guarantee of all essential qualifications. Whether that test is a wise one, or all that is essential, will be seen hereafter, but this does not affect the present argument one way or the other; it is the test which the British public has accepted and then, through negligence, allowed to be evaded.

The causes of this state of affairs are almost entirely economic. Either the expenses involved in obtaining a degree, even at a non-resident University such as London, are too great for the majority of those men and women who desire to be teachers, or else the salaries paid to the majority of teachers are not sufficient to attract men and women who have qualified for a university degree. In either case, and each is true, the public, when once it awakes to the need of providing fully qualified educators for its children, will have in some form or another to assist the teaching profession financially.

This future burden on the public might, however, be lightened, and at the same time a grave injustice remedied, if all scholarships provided by pious benefactors to enable poor students to obtain the best university education were restored to their original purpose. A blot on our national pride would also thus be removed; for foreign nations are inclined to wonder how wealthy English parents can accept the pecuniary assistance offered by such scholarships. But before the public will consent to take any steps in this matter they must be provided with accurate statistics as to the qualifications of secondary teachers. This in itself would be sufficient reason for the speedy formation of a teachers' register. But there are other and equally urgent reasons to be noticed.

Elsewhere I have remarked,[1] in discussing the qualifications of German secondary teachers, that the success of the teacher may be said to depend on three things—his knowledge of the subjects he teaches, his personality, and his acquaintance with the science of education. In England we have hitherto relied mainly on the first two of these, and have consequently among many failures produced a certain number of brilliant empiricists. The Germans, on the other hand, have attached

[1] *Special Reports on Educational Subjects*, vol. iii. paper 10. (Eyre and Spottiswoode.)

REGISTRATION OF TEACHERS 91

equal importance to all three, and to ensure the last have insisted on every teacher undergoing a course of professional training. Of the three qualifications personality must certainly stand first. Those qualities which distinguish and characterise a person are precisely those which inspire the teaching of the born schoolmaster with the vital force necessary to raise it to an educative influence. But even born teachers, and they can never form more than a small fraction of the profession, cannot afford to be ignorant of the work of their greatest predecessors, or to neglect to learn how to put their natural gift into practice. "True ease in writing comes from art, not chance," said a born poet; and the principle is even more applicable to the teacher, for in his case clumsiness in the practice of his art does not merely shock the ears of the public; it leaves an indelible trace on the minds and hearts of his pupils, and plays havoc with that mental and moral development on which the future of the nation depends. To allow teachers to learn their art by shutting them up in a room with a class for so many hours a day, without guidance and often without encouragement, is to ignore one of the most solemn of our responsibilities to future generations. To their credit be it said, secondary teachers themselves have been among the foremost in pressing their need of training on the attention of the people.

We may therefore conclude that, in its own interests, the nation must insist on the attainment by all secondary teachers of a certain standard of scholarship, of a knowledge of the principles which underlie their art, and of skill in its practice, before they can be recognised as fully qualified. To decide under what conditions such training can best be provided, without crushing personality and reducing all teachers to one dead mechanical level, is doubtless one of the most important as well as difficult duties of the Consultative Committee. The training of elementary teachers proves sufficiently that such a complex and delicate problem cannot be solved by the administrative mind. Here, again, it may be remarked in passing, the Consultative Committee might employ its influence to remove some of the fetters which weigh so heavily on the elementary teacher.

Before any attempts, however, can be made to provide training for our secondary teachers, it must be known what qualifications are possessed by existing schoolmasters, and what position these are to hold with regard to the new trained teachers; for it is certain that, although they may have gained their skill at the expense of their pupils, there are many brilliant and most successful men and women in their ranks. Again we come back to the need for the speedy formation of a teachers' register. And lastly, by this means better than any other, if, as it certainly will be, the register is made public, can the eyes of parents first be opened to the very inferior quality of much of the education provided for their children, and thus the cases of fraud and imposture, alluded to in a previous chapter, be duly exposed. How, then, are the qualifications of secondary teachers to be registered?

REGISTRATION OF TEACHERS

In the first place, their attainments in scholarship can be measured by their university degree, or by the examinations they have passed, and failing either, by the success obtained by their pupils at any recognised examinations; and any public evidence of their scholarship, such as literary or scientific work, should not be ignored. Their knowledge of the art of teaching, and their skill in its practice, are more difficult to register. Some few secondary teachers have already obtained teaching diplomas at a university or from the College of Preceptors; in their case the matter is easy enough. But the vast majority of schoolmasters can provide no evidence of these qualifications beyond experience, and this will have to be carefully recorded. It may, or rather must be taken for granted that a schoolmaster, who has spent many years in a good school or schools, is a good teacher. But here is the great difficulty, because at present there is no recognised means of distinguishing good schools from bad. If, however, the record of experience is to have any value, some such means must be devised. Otherwise teachers who have gradually sunk to, or never risen above, the level of those pseudo-secondary schools which, it is an open secret, furnish nothing more than a very inferior kind of elementary education, will rank in the public eye as high as those who have performed the same length of service in a school of the highest efficiency. It is evident, therefore, that before all existing teachers can be satisfactorily registered, existing secondary schools must be classified according to their efficiency and aim. In short, the first step towards a register of teachers is the formation of a register of schools. This implies inspection of all secondary schools.

Elementary teachers have, through the voice of their powerful political organisation, demanded that they should be included in the teachers' register. If the register states clearly all the qualifications I have named, not the slightest objection can be raised to granting this demand. Indeed, it would do much good for teachers of all the three branches of education to be united in this manner, and thus reminded that they possess one common national aim, which can never be attained so long as a spirit of rivalry and jealousy interferes with their co-operation.

CHAPTER VIII.

INSPECTION AND EXAMINATION OF SECONDARY SCHOOLS

IN the last chapter we have seen that, before a register of teachers, which is to have any real value, can be provided, it will be necessary to form a register of schools classified according to their efficiency and aim. When considering on an earlier page the actual resources for secondary education, we saw that it would be a grave injustice to existing schools, and an unpardonable waste of public money, for the Board to found, or to allow to be founded, new schools, without having first inquired into the actual supply and having learnt how far it meets, or how far it is capable of being improved so as to meet, the national need; and that such an inquiry must be directed towards ascertaining how many of these schools are really secondary and how many are efficient. Thus, starting from two different points, we have arrived at the same conclusion, namely, that the first undertaking of the Board must be the creation of a register of schools. It is needless to add that both registers, each throwing light on the other, are essential to a proper estimation of the value of our resources for secondary education. How, then, are the aim and efficiency of existing schools to be determined by the Board?

Some guarantee of both has been furnished by most private schools, and by struggling local endowed schools, compelled to satisfy the public on whose support they depend; they have been obliged to submit to an outside test, and, from the very nature of the obligation, to compete with other schools in satisfying this test. The most common of these have been the Oxford and Cambridge Local Examinations and those of the Oxford and Cambridge Joint Board and the College of Preceptors. The public has been gradually led to gauge the efficiency of these schools by their success in preparing their pupils for such examinations. Now, there is no doubt that the tests thus provided have been really valuable, in that they have obliged schools to maintain a certain standard of instruction, and it must immediately be granted that those which are successful in preparing for the Cambridge Junior and Senior Local Examinations, for instance, are secondary in so far as their course of instruction is concerned. To utterly condemn these examinations, as appears to be the fashion of the moment, is hardly just or wise. But whether they have proved a boon to education, as distinct from instruction, is another matter.

The head masters and head mistresses of many private schools complain that all their higher aims have to be subordinated to that of preparing pupils for written examinations; and the greater the stress of competition with other schools, the more completely must they sacrifice their educational ideals

INSPECTION OF SCHOOLS

to "cramming" of a more or less deleterious nature. Those consider themselves fortunate who, free from any dangerous competition, can dispense with these examinations altogether. Even were the acquisition of knowledge the sole end of education, and there is little doubt that it is in this mistaken belief that many parents approve of the tests we are considering, this system would not be free from blame; for not the worst evil of "cramming" is that knowledge so acquired, either by children or adults, is ephemeral; a still greater evil is that when a school depends for public support on its examination successes the teachers are sorely tempted to neglect dull or backward pupils in favour of those of higher promise. In short, nothing could be further removed from the best traditions of secondary education; and I have not the least hesitation in saying that there is no small number of private schools which have never attempted to satisfy this test, and yet are providing their pupils with education of the very highest order. Some other test must therefore be applied by the Board of Education; examination in the sense which it has acquired in connection with secondary schools must be supplemented, but not as some persons advocate supplanted, by inspection.

It is evident that this first inspection which will be necessary for the formation of a register of schools will not be a very expensive undertaking, nor one calling for the creation of a considerable staff of inspectors. A few men and women, having had long and recent experience in secondary schools, distinguished by the highest ability as teachers, satisfying the most exacting demands as to their qualifications, and at the same time possessing a wide knowledge of the various aims of English education, could, without much difficulty, be selected as inspectors by the Consultative Committee. To them might be added one or two persons with special knowledge as to the teaching of special subjects. Much time would not be required in order to enable them to visit all the secondary schools in the country, with the exception of those whose efficiency was already definitely established, and to report on them in sufficient detail to decide their position in the first register. Such a register could only be preliminary; for the decision arrived at, especially in the case of schools which were discovered to be below the standard essential, but which might yet be able to rise to it within a reasonable time if properly encouraged, could hardly be anything but provisional. And this inspection itself could only be regarded as a preliminary step. The ultimate object to be attained by inspection is far higher than that of forming a mere register of schools and of thus furnishing information immediately requisite.

Not the least important is to counteract some of the evils which increase of competition has necessarily introduced into all our secondary schools. To turn now to the public and local endowed schools, which might appear to be above the dangers of competition. So long as parents regard education as a direct preparation for life, which it should undoubtedly be, and so long as competitive examinations guard the entrance to many of the favourite paths of life, those schools which are most successful in passing boys and girls through those examinations will, other things being equal, continue to enjoy the largest share of public favour. There is little doubt, therefore, that even in our highest secondary schools the same evils are found in this respect as in the smaller schools already referred to, but, it must be admitted, in an attenuated form. The examinations they chiefly prepare for being such as can only be passed by boys and girls at the end of their school course, the effects are probably not so marked in the education of their younger pupils. But it cannot be denied that where schools prepare directly and in rivalry with other schools for competitive examinations, a tendency will invariably be found to neglect the duller and more backward pupils; and it is interesting to notice in this connection how carefully Germany has shielded her secondary schools from such influences.

The raising of the age for admission to many of the posts in the Civil Service has certainly done much to remove this temptation from the path of secondary schools; but the competition for money prizes offered by or to be held at the Universities, to say nothing of the doubtful morality of allowing the children of the rich to win these scholarships and exhibitions, is doubtless one of the most fatal stumbling-blocks to education in many schools, and particularly in the local endowed schools. Were these prizes redirected to their original object and granted to poor students alone, it cannot be doubted that a far larger number of the pupils of our secondary schools would proceed to the Universities, and thereby raise the educational level of the whole nation.

There are people who suggest that many of these evils would be obviated were a State "leaving examination" instituted for all secondary schools, as in Germany. It is difficult to see, unless we were to adopt the whole German organisation, how the spirit of competition between different schools, with its attendant drawbacks, would be reduced by this means. Those who support such a proposal should remember that a State leaving examination would inevitably crush that variety and freedom which have distinguished our secondary schools in the past; and, taking a wide survey of all these forces which have moulded and are still directing our national development, or pondering the looseness or flexibility of our constitution itself, they should pause and ask themselves if it is not to this very freedom, variety, and elasticity of our secondary education that, in spite of all its faults, we owe in great measure our present position in the world.

Some of our examinations certainly might be dispensed with; the tendency, even on the part of our older Universities, to impose them on very young children should be checked; and the character of all but a few must be radically reformed. But in its main features the system will continue. The mistake we have made in the past is not so much in accepting examinations as a test, as in considering them to be an all-sufficient test of efficiency. We have thus failed, as we failed in the past organisation of our central authorities, to foresee the abuses which must inevitably arise if one interest is encouraged without safeguarding others which it might undermine.

Written examinations at their best are not an all-sufficient test of education, nor even of instruction, but merely of the knowledge possessed by the candidate at a given moment. And even as such, under existing conditions they are only applied to a small fraction of the pupils in a school. If it is necessary that any test should be imposed, in the interests of the public, on our schools—and this can no longer be doubted—it should at least be one which reaches every pupil and attempts to cover the whole range of education. Inspection alone can satisfy these two conditions.

If we consider the various influences that have characterised secondary education in the past, we must admit that those which have told directly on the formation of character have been the most useful to the nation. While, however, character must form the foundation of all the qualities essential to men and women in the modern struggle for existence, the conviction is dawning on the people that greater attention should be paid in our secondary schools to the training of the intelligence. But, as we have seen, there still exists an inclination to attach exaggerated importance to the acquisition of knowledge as an end in itself. Nevertheless, if the people of England could only be persuaded to listen to the leading exponents of pedagogical science—the most discredited of all theorists in this country—at any rate a compromise might be effected; and while demanding on their side that a certain standard of knowledge should be attained in all secondary schools, the people would allow that the methods of instruction by which this standard is attained must either promote or check intellectual development.

We may consequently conclude that the inspector, who has to test the efficiency of a secondary school, has not so much to concern himself with the standard of knowledge attained—except in the case of those pupils who do not present themselves for examination—but rather to observe the methods of instruction employed. A no less important part of his duties will be to weigh all the different educational influences which surround the pupils. Arbitrary distinctions cannot be drawn between these influences; they include everything from the size and equipment of a classroom to the moral tone which pervades the whole school organism.

To be capable of weighing all these influences, some of a very subtle nature rarely appreciated by those who have not experienced their power, evidently demands exceptional qualifications on the part of the inspector; and certainly he cannot afford to be without a very wide knowledge of the most modern developments in what may be termed the material side of the educational environment. "The schoolhouse of the young soul," said Jean Paul Richter, "does not merely consist of lecture and lesson rooms, but also of the school ground, the sleeping-room, the eating-room, the playground, the staircase, and of every place."

So far we have only regarded the inspector as a passive observer and recorder. He must be far more than this. He has an active mission to perform, that of raising secondary education to the highest possible realisation of English and, as far as the two are compatible, of foreign ideals. His own experience as a schoolmaster, provided that it is of recent date, must be placed at the disposal of all teachers with whom he comes into contact; to them he will stand in the position of a severely friendly critic, but at the same time of one who is ever ready to encourage and help rather than to blame, and careful not to discourage through any want of tact in dealing with that most sensitive and highly-strung of all creatures—the secondary schoolmaster. Tact, of all things, will be most necessary; pressure must be applied gradually and diplomatically; and by the time the inspector has thus led teachers to welcome his visits he will himself have acquired a new usefulness in his mission. For during this time he will have been accumulating educational experience from his inspectorial visitations; in many schools he will have found special points of excellence, in others he will have traced the causes of failure and weakness. All these he will be able to make known to the schools within his province, and thus do more than can be done by any other means to bring the best English influences to bear on the development of our secondary education.

It is the conviction that in this respect can the inspector be most useful which has caused all educationists to welcome the decision of the great public schools to open their doors to inspection. In its choice of inspectors may the Board of Education do nothing to close these open doors! But at the same time it is sincerely to be hoped that in extending the power of inspection to "any university or other organisation" the Board will insist on the possession of the irreducible minimum of qualifications by all inspectors whom these bodies may appoint.

The opinion as to this minimum of those masters in secondary schools who are willing to be inspected should not be ignored, and the Board of Education should strive to satisfy the demands embodied in a resolution recently passed by that increasingly representative body—the Assistant Masters' Association—to the effect that, in secondary schools, inspection should be compulsory, the cost borne by the Board of Education, and that the inspectors should have had at least five years' recent experience in similar schools.

CHAPTER IX.

THE BOARD OF EDUCATION AND WELSH SECONDARY SCHOOLS

IT will be noticed that in the Board of Education Act it is expressly stated that the inspection of schools, established under the Welsh Intermediate Education Act, 1889, shall continue to be carried out as heretofore. This special provision calls for some explanation.

The Board of Education having been appointed to control primary and technical as well as secondary education, it is impossible, for administrative reasons, even if desirable, immediately to create separate central authorities for England and Wales. But it should not be forgotten that secondary education is in a more advanced state of organisation in the Principality than in England. Neither must the fact be lost sight of that the forces which presided over its development in Wales are so different from those which, as far as can be conjectured, will determine its future in this country; the social, religious, and economic conditions which its organisation must satisfy are so distinct from those of England, and, at the same time, so much more clearly defined, that it would be impossible to provide a system of control, common in all details, which would meet the two classes of requirements. A brief survey of the history and organisation of secondary or—to use the more common term—intermediate education in Wales will probably establish this view of the case.

Past attempts to deal with the organisation of secondary education apart from the other branches failed in England chiefly owing to the lack of any strong public feeling as to the inefficiency of the actual supply. While fully alive to the advantages which our industry and commerce may derive from technical instruction, the people have not, during recent years, felt the need of those intellectual and moral benefits which it is the particular province of secondary education to bestow. In Wales it has been otherwise, and during the last decade we have witnessed an educational revival to which, perhaps, the only parallels in history are to be found in connection with Prussia after her overthrow by Napoleon, and, in a more limited sense, with France after the disasters of 1870.

But the motives which have produced the educational zeal of the Welsh are of even a higher nature than the desire, tinged with revenge, for the recovery of national status. In 1847 reports were published by three commissioners, who had been appointed by the Committee of Council on Education to inquire into the state of education in Wales. No official documents have denounced more strongly educational inefficiency, with its attendant intellectual and moral evils. The conditions of life and morals among the lower industrial and agricultural classes were painted in the darkest colours. Whether the picture was exaggerated or not, the resentment which it aroused was of a healthy kind, and ultimately evolved a universal desire for national moral and intellectual regeneration. Public feeling was not satisfied until the passing of the Welsh Intermediate Education Act in 1889.

The progress which has been made since that date attests the latent force which had accumulated during the period devoted to the promotion of legislation. Not that it must be imagined that the country had been idle in other directions. In the meantime the University of Wales had been established, a few new secondary schools had arisen, and the old grammar schools had been resuscitated by the Charity Commissioners under the Endowed Schools Acts. But the Charity Commissioners' laborious process of making schemes for the administration of existing endowments, while tolerated in England, where there was no strong popular demand for new secondary schools, could hardly be expected to satisfy a people hungering after increased educational facilities.

It is doubtless owing to the relative supineness of public opinion in England that Parliament has not yet sanctioned a complete scheme for the organisation of secondary education in this country, while it did so ten years ago for Wales. For it is fully recognised that no scheme can be successful which does not largely depend on local government. But while it is a safe thing to entrust secondary education to local authorities, representing men and women determined to use it as a means of raising the moral and intellectual tone of the community, it is a dangerous thing to commit it to the control of others who are incapable of appreciating its highest aims, or who show a willingness to divert it to inferior ends. The duty of a Government which has the true interests of the nation at heart is perfectly clear in either case. In the former it is only necessary to aid the people to work out their own salvation, to remove all obstacles in their way, and, if one may employ the figure, to hold the reins firmly in the hand so as to be ready to guide should guidance be necessary; in the latter the people must be aroused to their need of salvation, and encouraged to help themselves, but the Government must undertake to provide them with the best advice, and to prevent them from following any other. There were many difficulties, however, in the way of entrusting intermediate education to local government in Wales, until the Act of 1888 established local authorities of a suitable kind in the form of County Councils.

The Welsh Intermediate Education Act, 1889, constituted educational authorities, termed Joint Education Committees, for each county and county borough. These committees each consist of five persons, three nominated by the County (or County Borough) Council and two by the Lord President, it being required that the two should be "persons well acquainted with the conditions of Wales and the wants of the people." It was the first duty of the committees to submit to the Charity

Commissioners schemes for the intermediate and technical education of the inhabitants within their areas. The procedure which must be followed under the Endowed Schools Acts before schemes can be finally approved appears to be unnecessarily elaborate and prolonged, and probably all such procedure will be simplified by the new Board of Education.

According to the information supplied by the Charity Commissioners, the following was the fate of the seventeen schemes proposed by the Joint Education Committees.[1] In seven cases, owing to disagreements between the Charity Commissioners and the committees, the original schemes of the latter were submitted to the Education Department, as alternative schemes to those of the Charity Commissioners, and four of them were preferred by the department. After seventeen schemes had been approved by the department nine of them were, in consequence of petitions, laid before Parliament; with the result that six were amended. The whole business occupied about five years.

It will thus be seen that though the Charity Commissioners may be regarded, in a sense, as the central authority for Welsh intermediate education, their power is limited. But the fact remains that, having presided over the earliest development of the new organisation, they are the only body possessing a practical acquaintance with the peculiar requirements of the Welsh people. It is, therefore, to be hoped that, when the Board of Education takes over the educational func-

---

[1] See *Special Reports on Educational Subjects*, vol. ii. (Eyre and Spottiswoode, 1898.)

tions of the Charity Commissioners, as it is in every way desirable that it should do, it will also incorporate in its staff those persons who have been most successfully employed in the exercise of these functions. For thus alone can the danger be avoided of attempting to force English and Welsh education along a common line of development in the future. To entrust Welsh intermediate education to the control of a *personnel* inspired by the traditions of English education, would be hardly less fatal than to hand over the destinies of English secondary education to the care of a department composed of, or unduly influenced by, men who were accustomed to the methods of organisation necessitated by the peculiar requirements of Welsh intermediate education. But this is not the point which has raised the anxiety of Welsh educationists. That can be elucidated only by the consideration of certain financial details.

It was evident that no amount of organisation would really further progress unless money could be supplied to meet the expenses which had to be incurred in creating new schools and in remodelling the old. Permission was therefore given by the Act to the Joint Education Committees to insert in their schemes, on the recommendation of the County Council, "provision for a payment for the purposes of the scheme out of the county rate to an amount not exceeding a halfpenny in the pound." The Technical Instruction Act, 1889, gave County Councils, County Borough Councils, and Urban Sanitary Authorities the power to levy a rate of a penny in the pound for the same purpose; and the Local Taxation (Customs and Excise) Act, 1890, placed a considerable sum of money at the disposal of the County Councils, with the permission, in the case of Wales, to apply it to intermediate and not only to technical education, as in England. But it is the Treasury grant which has produced the most important results from a purely educational point of view. For this grant, which must not exceed the amount payable out of the rates, is awarded on the following, among other, conditions: (*a*) The school must be efficient as regards instruction; (*b*) its premises must be healthy and suitable for the purposes of an intermediate school; (*c*) its premises must provide sufficient accommodation for the scholars attending the school; (*d*) it must be supplied with suitable furniture and apparatus; and (*e*) it must be conducted in accordance with the scheme under which it is established.

"For the purpose of ascertaining whether these conditions are fulfilled," say the Regulations, "there shall be an annual examination and inspection of the school." It may be judged from the above stipulations what is meant by inspection in Wales.

Now, the Joint Education Committees had certain misgivings as to this inspection. They feared that, if it was undertaken by the Treasury, an inflexible code might be imposed on the new secondary schools, in much the same way as has been done by the Education Department for elementary schools. They felt that if this inspection was to be of real benefit to education, it should be carried out by a body fully cognisant of the different local requirements. All the Joint Education Committees, therefore, submitted identical proposals to the Charity Commissioners for the establishment of a Central Welsh Board of Intermediate Education, which should act as the agent of the Treasury for the purposes of inspection. On the 18th of June, 1891, a deputation waited on Mr. Goschen, who was then Chancellor of the Exchequer, to urge the passing of this proposal. A year later it was agreed to, on condition that the Charity Commissioners should exercise the same supervisory powers over the Board's inspection as they do under the Endowed Schools Acts over the examination of endowed schools in England. Presiding as it does over the county governing bodies and other sections of the local organisation, to which it is impossible at present to do more than refer, this central Welsh Board is little less than the central educational authority for Wales. But it must not be imagined that the central government allows it complete freedom. The fact which it is important to notice here is, that Wales possesses a system of inspection which has proved most successful in promoting the interests of education.

A system of inspection no less thorough is, as we have seen, demanded by the majority of schoolmasters in England; and though the Board of Education may not immediately establish such a system, the third clause of the Act marks its inception But at the same time this clause, being of an entirely permissive nature, would have seriously interfered with the existing arrangements under the

Central Welsh Board, and the desire of Welsh educationists that a new system of inspection might not be imposed on their schools is not to be wondered at.

The Welsh organisation for inspection would not be suitable to England, but that fact affords no justification for interfering with the very interesting educational movement which is proceeding in the Principality. All who are interested in the future of democracy will watch that movement with the closest attention. It is yet too soon to predict its success, but the earnestness which has characterised its beginning can only command admiration.

CHAPTER X.

LOCAL AUTHORITIES FOR SECONDARY EDUCATION

THE whole question of democratic local government is one which is exercising the minds of all thoughtful people. There is a strong party in England which denies the very principles on which it is based, which considers that if rating or property qualifications are not imposed on those who vote rates or govern property their powers should be very strictly limited, local government being beyond everything else "a machine for raising and employing money." Such a party may be termed reactionary, but there is nothing to be gained by ignoring the fact that it numbers more confessed adherents to-day than ten or even five years ago. It is necessary to draw attention to these considerations here, because many educationists, who have approached the problems of central government with caution and modesty, treat the thorny question of local authorities for secondary education with utter indifference to the strong and serious opposition displayed towards any extension of the functions of local government, as at present established. But it must be admitted that even some of the most strenuous advocates of the policy of immediately entrusting secondary education

LOCAL AUTHORITIES 115

to the care of County Councils, now hesitate before the recently avowed determination of some of the leading members of these bodies, to ignore all traditions in the founding of new schools under their direction.

This is not the place to do more than record these aspects of the question. But it is well to know, before pursuing a path with a light heart, that there are people who fear to tread it. Not that we can retrace our steps—a country cannot walk back on its own history; but we may at least keep a sharp look out for pitfalls. We may take warning from the fate of one of the boldest members of the present Government, who in 1896 sacrificed that very prestige which made him of the greatest service to the cause of education, by a bad fall along this same path leading to local authorities for secondary education; but that is no reason why the Government should not pursue its way; there is all the greater need for it to march warily forward and complete the good work it has begun in the Board of Education Act.

In the last chapter I referred to the attitude of the Welsh people towards secondary education, and showed that the great force which was behind the educational revival in Wales was a united desire for moral and intellectual regeneration. Where such a force exists it should be allowed the freest play; it certainly affords a justification for entrusting secondary education to local control of the most democratic nature. In England, however, the people, or perhaps it would be more correct to say their representatives on various local bodies, have been divided into three distinct and opposing camps—one consisting of a small remnant supporting the moral, another advocating the intellectual, and the largest and most influential refusing to recognise anything but the utilitarian aim of education.[1] We have seen that it was the attack on the first, and the schools they defended, which started the movement among the more thoughtful of the community that has culminated in the establishment of the Board of Education.

If, thirty years ago, before the creation of School Boards, the advice of the Schools Inquiry Commission had been followed, there is little doubt that the local authorities which they recommended might have brought the goodwill of the people to bear with great success on the solution of the problems of higher education. But now things are otherwise; the deplorable division of opinion alluded to above is only one of the results of strictly confining the enthusiasm of local authorities to elementary and technical education alone. The majority of educationists will at present allow nothing but the most practical considerations to weigh, and it may be immediately admitted that they weigh very heavily, in favour of the speedy establishment of local authorities empowered to deal with secondary education.

[1] I have not referred to a fourth class, so utterly indifferent to education of any kind that, when large sums of money were placed at the disposal of local authorities for the support of technical education, it persuaded some of these bodies to apply this money to the reduction of the rates.

To these, local authorities appear indispensable as "machines for raising and employing money." The School Boards, as is well known, have powers of drawing on the rates, practically to an unlimited extent, in support of elementary schools under their protection; they have recently used these powers for the promotion of higher-grade education, and thus, as we have seen, entered into direct competition with secondary schools. County Councils and County Borough Councils have not only had a considerable sum of money placed at their disposal for the encouragement of technical education, but also possess, together with District Councils, the right of raising a rate of one penny in the pound for the same purpose. How these councils have, under the direction of the Science and Art Department, influenced local endowed schools has already been related.

Secondary education, consequently, stands alone in having no "machine for raising and employing money" in its behalf. How is this want to be supplied?

While the Board of Education Bill was being drafted one of the difficulties which must have arisen was, without doubt, in connection with the clause providing for the inspection of any secondary schools "desiring to be so inspected." How were the numerous poverty-stricken schools to meet the expense of satisfying this desire? The riddle was solved by adding a subsection to the clause empowering County and County Borough Councils to pay for the inspection of any schools within their areas "out of any money applicable for the purposes of technical education." Here, then, is a definitely established precedent for regarding County and County Borough Councils as the future machines for raising and employing money on behalf of secondary education. And, indeed, no local bodies are more suitable.

School Boards are out of the question, if only on the ground that they are an anachronism in that great system of local government partially re-established by the Conservatives in the Local Government Act of 1888, and by the Liberals in the Act of 1894. School Boards are a survival of the days of *ad hoc* authorities, when the map of England was redrafted by Government clerks to meet various demands as they arose. The County Council system, on the other hand, is not only adapted to those localities which divide between them the whole area of England, and within which influences peculiar to each have throughout centuries moulded distinctive features of thought and habit; it not only, by recognising the independence of great towns, takes into account those modern forces which have united a varied population in large industrial and commercial centres; but, besides conforming to these axioms of local government, it is gradually concentrating scattered administrative functions in one central local body. In spite of all the excellent work which the School Boards have done, they cannot continue to exist much longer, even for the work of elementary education, in face of the imperative demand of modern times for simplicity of organisation and economy of effort. Sentiment cannot even come to their rescue, for the long-dormant sentiment of locality has been reawakened to overcome all others. The future of local government lies in the system re-established in 1888 and 1894.

The county must be considered, at any rate for educational purposes, as the unit of this system. We have seen, nevertheless, that, as far as technical education is concerned, the right of *raising* money has been allowed also to District Councils, which by the Act of 1894 have been brought into "definite relationship to the county and to the county authority."[1] But they are practically without the power of *employing* this money, and we find that they therefore are devoting it to the support of the general scheme of the whole county. Here we have another most important precedent; its value becomes immediately evident from the consideration of certain conditions affecting the supply of secondary education.

To take a basis of calculation which meets with general acceptance, it may be said that twenty-five per thousand of the population require secondary education. As it is doubtful if many more than one-third of this number are at present receiving it, it will certainly be many years before the desired level is attained.[2] But to raise the supply so as to satisfy

[1] LAURENCE GOMME, *Principles of Local Government*, p. 19. (Archibald Constable and Co., 1897.)

[2] It may be calculated that in Prussia about 10·2 per 1,000 of the *male* population were educated in the State secondary schools in 1895. In calculating these figures I have been unable to take private schools, perhaps not so numerous as is generally imagined, into account. The figures for England do include private schools.

the needs of twenty-five per thousand of the population will be the chief object of local authorities; indeed, this will be their *raison d'être*. Evidently, therefore, local authorities will be responsible for a large number of new secondary schools in the future.

Now, it would be ridiculous to impose laws on the people, obliging them to send their children to secondary schools within the boundaries of their own parishes or districts. To say nothing of the great public schools, which do not enter into the local authority problem, the desire, whether altogether wise or not, of parents to send their sons and daughters to boarding schools, not necessarily or by any means generally in a different county, is too deeply rooted in English custom to be disregarded in the new organisation. Furthermore, unless all healthy rivalry between schools is to be crushed, even supposing religious differences were ignored in secondary education, parents will still continue to consult their own special tastes, and will willingly pay small daily travelling expenses to procure, what appear to them, advantages should the schools of their choice be at a considerable distance from their doors.

Neither must it be forgotten that local prejudices within small areas, if represented on an authoritative body—which might more easily happen when that body is not elected for educational purposes only—would prove fatal to much admirable private enterprise, even if the powers of that body were reduced to a minimum. No thoughtful person will deny that the work of secondary education is of so delicate a nature, and at the same time of such supreme importance to the nation, that it must be shielded from all external friction.

These considerations in themselves afford sufficient reason for regarding the County (or County Borough) Council area as the smallest within which a local authority should direct the employment of money raised for secondary education. If the minor councils were represented on the educational committee of the County Councils, not only might the employment, but also the raising of money be directed within the county area by the larger body. But here we touch on one of the most difficult administrative problems to be solved in connection with the establishment of local authorities. The rating area must, of course, be determined by community of educational interests. But, as anyone knows who has witnessed the attempts of a growing county borough to incorporate outlying districts, there is nothing more difficult than to persuade people of community of interest when its acknowledgment implies responsibilities of a very practical nature.

It may be safely predicted, for instance, that many a parish or district, many a large town flourishing within the limits of population decreed for a non-county borough, would gladly take advantage of the facilities afforded by a technical school supported by the rates of a neighbouring county borough. Or, to take another example of what might easily happen from a too strict demarcation of educational areas, a group of small county boroughs might be in urgent need of a technical or other school of university rank, and yet no one of them might be sufficiently rich to support such an institution alone.

Even the problem itself cannot be fully stated in a work of the present scope; but it may safely be said that the key to its solution, whether it take the form of one authority for all areas capable of supporting an institution of university rank, or of the combination of a number of smaller local authorities when the interests of such an institution are concerned, is to be found in an appeal to that spirit of locality, hardly less strong within its natural limits than that of nationality, but nevertheless so universally ignored in the creation of the factitious School Board areas. It would be far better to place all institutions of the rank referred to directly under the central authority than to interfere in any way with the deep-rooted sentiment of locality; for on its preservation depends the success of the whole of local government in its many and varied aspects.

When we come to the powers which will be demanded by the local authorities in return for the voting and expenditure of local money, we are face to face with a question of the gravest importance. To give them the power of inspecting secondary schools within their areas would cause a revolt among all existing schools. After what I have already said concerning inspection, there is no need to insist further on the very high qualifications which will be required of inspectors; and high qualifications mean high salaries. It would, of course, be useless to employ men and women to inspect the teaching

LOCAL AUTHORITIES

of subjects of which they knew nothing, or had had no experience in teaching. Are any County Councils prepared therefore to support the staff of inspectors which would be necessary, or would the small amount of work that each staff would have to perform justify the expenditure of public money involved? The lamentable results of the necessary considerations of economy, displayed by the Technical Instruction Committees of some County Councils in their choice of inspectors, should prove a terrible warning to those who have hitherto believed that inspection should be left in the hands of local authorities. Surely no one will any longer venture to deny that the Consultative Committee is the only body in the new organisation which is competent to select inspectors for secondary schools. In devolving powers on local authorities the Board of Education cannot afford to overlook the fact that, however great and valuable a part County Councils are to play in guiding the future destinies of this country, they are at present but learning the art of governing; and while it is doubtless necessary that they should experiment on some branches of national life, our existence as a nation depends too intimately on the speedy organisation of secondary education to allow us to run any risks, or to lose a single step in the race in which the foreigner is already pressing us so hard.

CHAPTER XI.

THE NATION'S OPPORTUNITY

THE British Empire may be said to rest on the foundations of character and wealth. Innumerable and ever-changing forces have doubtless contributed to the rearing of this mighty fabric, but on these foundations its existence depends. Perhaps the figure would be more accurately drawn if we were to regard character as the bedrock supporting the foundation of wealth; but it might then convey a false impression, the term "bedrock" implying something of a fixed and unalterable nature, whereas I must postulate at the outset that the English character not only owes a vast amount of its strength to our past education, but that the school of the future may deform and debase it.

It may perhaps be objected that wealth is a minor consideration beside character; that the latter has in our history always produced and will continue to produce the former. But I think that such an objection would arise from failure to read the modern world aright, a fault which is not less dangerous to our national supremacy than the obliquity of vision which causes some of our countrymen to overlook all but the material sources of our greatness.

There is no need to repeat here that the formation of character was, and still is in our great public schools, the supreme end of English education. The benefits which such education has conferred on the nation may be judged from the fact that even yet character plays a greater part in our legislative and executive government than in those of any other countries.

There are not a few keen observers, however, who tell us that in this respect each lowering of the suffrage has caused a marked deterioration in Parliament. It would indeed be strange if it had been otherwise. Had the course of progress been foreseen with unerring vision, or had extensions of the franchise been the outcome of a sincere conviction of the justice of universal suffrage, and not merely moves in the party game, we might wonder now that our governing classes, before admitting a lower order to the privileges which they had so long monopolised, did not prepare it by education for its new responsibilities. There were, indeed, prophets before 1870 to foretell the fate that must befall a country, millions of whose inhabitants were uneducated. "If the whole English People, during these 'twenty years of respite,'" thundered Carlyle in 1847, "be not educated, with at least schoolmaster's educating, a tremendous responsibility, before God and men, will rest somewhere!"

It will be useful at this point to pause and ask ourselves what should have been the guiding principles of English education, if it had been provided for the lower classes with the express object of preparing them for admission to the government of the nation.

"Long after the sceptre of power had passed from the landed gentry to the middle classes," remarks Mr. Lecky, "the old belief, or prejudice, or superstition that the administration of government ought to be chiefly entrusted to gentlemen, prevailed, and, in spite of all democratic agitations, it is certainly very far from extinct."

And proceeding to analyse the causes underlying this belief, he continues :—

"The code of honour which the conventionalities of society attach to the idea of a gentleman is, indeed, a somewhat capricious thing, and certainly not co-extensive with the moral law. . . . At the same time, it is no less true that on special subjects, and within a restricted sphere, the code of honour of a gentleman is the most powerful of all restraining influences, more powerful even than religion with ordinary men. Whenever it pervades the public service men will soon learn to recognise that public servants cannot be bribed or corrupted; . . . that their word may be trusted, that they are not likely to act by tortuous or intriguing methods. The credit of England in the world depends largely upon this conviction, and that credit has been no small element of her prosperity."[1]

All that was best in the oligarchical government of the eighteenth and earlier nineteenth centuries was to be directly attributed to this code of honour, which our public schools still make it their chief object to maintain and perfect. To spread, if not the exact code of honour, at any rate its finest spirit, among the people; to adapt this guiding principle of the

---

[1] *Democracy and Liberty*, vol. i. 115 *sqq*. (Longmans and Co., 1896.)

THE NATION'S OPPORTUNITY

traditional education of our governing classes to the education of the classes about to be admitted to the responsibilities and privileges of government, would have been the only means of ensuring the unbroken continuation of the power of English character throughout the early years of the rise of democracy. Such would have been even a more imperative aim of education than the enlightenment of ignorance. For though it is doubtless true, as the distinguished authority whom I have just quoted remarks, "Ignorance in the elective body does not naturally produce ignorance in the representative body; it is much more likely to produce dishonesty"[1]—it is likewise true that the profoundest knowledge on the part of the electors will not prevent, without a high code of honour, the choice of dishonest representatives. And yet even after the event, after we had admitted masses of uneducated people to a share in the government, and were compelled to acknowledge their right to education, politicians of every type seem to have vied with one another in extolling knowledge, or even knowledge-producing machinery, as the god of education. The Elementary Education Acts and the Technical Instruction Acts show a consistent tendency to educate the people by raising up schools cut off from the influence of those which had in the past educated our governing classes, thus throwing all the best influences of past methods of government into a hopeless minority among the electors of Parliaments, County Councils, and all local authorities. "Know-

[1] *Democracy and Liberty*, vol. i. 115 *sqq.*

ledge!" cry the people; "Machinery!" cry the officials. Who hears the plea for "Character," for strengthening this old and ever-more-essential foundation of our empire? The man who ventures to preach the ethical side of education is dubbed a faddist, and if he be a departmental servant is silenced or discredited.

Nothing has contributed more to this neglect of the proper education of democracy than the fact that, while the schools established for the education of these classes admitted to the franchise during the present century are under the control of the State, those on the other hand whose special province it has always been to educate the governing classes have been allowed to remain outside of the State system. Thus we have had no national system of schools in the true sense. If proof is needed in support of this assertion it is afforded by the upward tendencies in the growth of the Board School system.

It was naturally to be expected that, when the indefeasible right of all ranks of the people to education was once for all recognised by the Act of 1870, the country would not long remain satisfied with the minimum of "schoolmaster's educating" then secured. Not only do we find the upper age limit of compulsory elementary education steadily being raised—though it must be confessed we are still behind the foremost Continental nations in this respect—but greater facilities for education higher than elementary being provided. Now, this upward growth beyond the elementary stage has been an interesting example of the self-education of uneducated classes, which presents, from the very collective nature combined with the social characteristics of the movement, greater defects than the self-education of the individual. Instead of shooting out branches into the secondary system already existing, the elementary schools preferred to push their own system, with all its faults of isolation and all its tendencies to confirm social inferiority through education, into unknown and unexplored regions. I do not for a moment mean to imply that the instruction of our higher primary schools is not very valuable to boys and girls who otherwise would be compelled to leave school at the age of twelve or thirteen; but it is dangerous to the interests of the nation in so far as it draws the children of poor parents from the secondary schools and is absolutely cut off from, or repels the influence of, the traditional education of the governing classes of the past. If the truth of what has gone before is admitted it will be willingly allowed that the Board of Education Act, in bringing secondary schools under the control of the State and into the national system, offers the nation an opportunity of raising democracy to a height of perfection which it has never yet attained. Will this opportunity be taken? will it be understood? If it is not to be lost, and nothing less than a revolution of the whole constitution can bring it round again, secondary schools must be brought into their right place in the very centre of the national system, to radiate without let or hindrance, on the younger schools developing around them, all the experience they have stored up, all the influences which they have perfected in the training of our greatest men, all the indelible traces of the great pupils and masters who have learnt and taught within them. We talk much just now of an educational ladder on which the poorest child may climb, if he can, from the elementary school to the university. That is a great and desirable thing, and is in itself a sufficient plea for a well-organised national system; but it is of prior importance to the nation that the true educational spirit, which is to be found underlying our traditions, should inspire every teacher, from the humblest classmaster to the most learned of professors. Beside this ideal the providing of knowledge-producing machinery is as nothing.

Having attempted to show the peculiar opportunity which is now offered for ensuring to democracy that basis of character on which the highest previous types of government have rested, let us consider how it may likewise be used for strengthening that foundation of wealth which is indispensable to the existence of our empire.

It has often been said that the greatest and best reforms have been produced in England by national poverty and distress. And though to-day there is probably less of either than at any time in our history, whatever popular support has been given to the recent efforts of the Intellectuals to found a national system of education, may be traced to the widespread conviction that foreign nations are pressing us more closely than ever in the race for existence. It is not

THE NATION'S OPPORTUNITY

until the race becomes fast and keenly contested that training and the cultivation of power and endurance begin to tell. So long as the rest of Europe was at war, or recovering from war, our natural powers, freed from certain economic restrictions imposed by legislation, were sufficient to place us easily at the head of all commercial and industrial enterprise. But for nearly thirty years the chief European nations, to say nothing of America, have been able to compete with us on equal terms. Germany and France, our two foremost rivals in commerce and industry, have been at peace, and, while spending less on their armies than ourselves, provide, through compulsory military service, a training to their young men which, whatever its drawbacks, is of undoubted value as a preparation for commercial and industrial pursuits; of such value, indeed, that many persons hold that it more than atones for the delay consequent in starting a career. France, owing to an incalculable extent to the subordination of the ethical to the intellectual aim in her education, has, it is true, so immeasurably weakened the moral foundations of her former greatness that little short of national regeneration will restore her to the position of a rival to be feared. With Germany, however, we have entered upon a contest which has taken the form of one of the keenest industrial and commercial competitions which the world has seen, and at the same time one of the most honourably conducted. Our people have observed with close attention the rapid strides which Germany has made in this competition, and, seeing the immediate relation of her success to education, have evinced an interest in the amount and quality of our educational supply which has never yet been equalled. When we think of the immense difficulties and the poverty against which Germany had to contend in adapting her education to modern requirements, we cannot but consider this opportunity of organising or reforming our schools as indeed golden since it comes at a moment of extraordinary prosperity and finds the people sensible of the dangers which await us in the future. What may be the fate of England and Germany before the fierce rush of competition which comes from the West with accelerating speed it is difficult to foretell. It seems most likely, however, that our destiny for some years to come is to serve one another as "pacemakers" in the race between Eastern and Western civilisation.

Education, directed towards the strengthening of the national foundations of wealth and considered for the moment *apart from the formation of character*, is concerned with the training of the intelligence through the acquisition of knowledge; the acquisition of knowledge being regarded rather as a means of intellectual development than as an end in itself. So that the subjects which are to be taught in our schools must satisfy two conditions: first and foremost they must in themselves be thoroughly effective as instruments of intellectual training; secondly, they should be of recognised utility in the battle of modern life. Furthermore, they should be handled by the teacher in such a manner as to produce the maximum of effect.

Hardly anyone will now venture to deny that elementary schools have better adapted their methods of teaching and their choice of subjects to the training of the intelligence than secondary schools; and the influence which the former may in their turn exercise over the latter, when both are brought into one national system, will be of inestimable value to our economic prosperity. On their combined efforts and the interchange of their best elements can alone be built up efficient technical education of all grades. I have attempted to show that national education has at the present moment two duties to fulfil, of all the greater importance now because they have been grievously neglected in the past. In a democracy such as ours we have always to remember that each school in the land is educating the governing classes of the future, and at the same time we cannot afford to forget that unless education equips us for the struggle for wealth the day may arrive when there is little to govern, and we may not even be allowed to govern that little ourselves. National independence is one of the most cherished prizes of the modern world, and it is nothing less than this which is staked on the present educational opportunity. One of the foremost writers on Imperial policy recently remarked:—

"The great need of our lives, and of the education which leads us into them is harmony, or oneness. The multitude of sporadic efforts, made at present either on a large scale by the nation in its various aspects or on a smaller scale by the schoolmaster in his divers compartments, require to be brought together, co-ordinated, and organised. The secret of harmony is unity of purpose. The meaning of organisation is the combination of efforts to one end."[1]

[1] SPENSER WILKINSON, *The Nation's Awakening*, p. 299. (Archibald Constable and Co., 1896.)

In these words Mr. Spenser Wilkinson lays bare the fundamental error of our education. "The present generation had its schooling in compartments," he remarks earlier. "History, geography, languages, and the sciences were taught by so many different teachers, each of them acting as though the other subjects and the other teachers had no existence." But before we can get this combination of efforts to one end, before we can unite teachers in the realisation that they are one and all "training British citizens," the people must first clearly perceive that all schools—primary, secondary, or technical—are, in conjunction with the Universities, performing a definite share of the work of national education. To each of these three kinds of school must be assigned its proper part, and it has now become the duty of the State to determine what this part is, and to see that each is fulfilled in a manner worthy of our great national responsibilities. This, in short, is the whole task of the Board of Education.

In the brief review which I have given of this task several duties stand out in marked prominence. At this point it may be well to collect in a short summary those which are the most pressing.

We have seen that the Board of Education must in the first place concentrate its attention on the Secondary Education Department. This department must open its career by taking a census of the existing supply of secondary schools; in other words, it must, with the least possible delay, form a register of the schools which are efficient or capable of being made efficient. At the commencement of this work it must be assisted by the Consultative Committee in establishing a provisional criterion of educational efficiency, in determining the irreducible intellectual minimum to be satisfied by instruction in various types of secondary schools, and in selecting inspectors who are competent to apply such standards of measurement.

The work will be made easier for the Secondary Education Department if existing local authorities are empowered, without prejudice to the ultimate constitution of the special authorities required, to aid in gathering information as to the existing supply of schools within their respective areas, and as to the peculiar local needs which those schools have or have not satisfied in the past. Any attempts to inquire into the religious instruction which is given in secondary schools must, at the outset, be sternly repressed, or the whole work is doomed to years of failure.

The standard by which these schools are to be judged must at first, for obvious reasons, be pitched lower than would appear to be strictly required by our national position; but the mission of the inspectors is gradually to raise them year by year, so that each annual register will mark a stage of progress accomplished towards the desired end. And it should be remembered that there is no turning back from this task when it is once begun; it must be pursued to the close of our history, until we drop out of the march of civilisation, and the desired end becomes a fixed and diminishing point.

The cost of forming the register of schools may, under the provisions of the Board of Education Act, be borne in its most serious item, that of inspection, by the local authorities just alluded to, who will be quick to perceive the advantage of possessing accurate and unbiassed information respecting the local supply of secondary education. The register will acquire additional value in their eyes from the fact that it furnishes an easy and reliable means of comparing the efforts of different localities.

Having formed a register of schools, the next step must be to form a register of teachers. Here, again, the standard of admission must at first be low, and must be gradually raised until we possess an army of highly qualified and trained teachers second to none in the world. It will be immediately discovered that there are serious gaps in their ranks which need filling with the least possible delay. I may refer especially to the want of a sufficient number of first-rate English teachers of modern languages. In this connection the Secondary Education Department will be brought into direct contact with the Universities, and if it commands their confidence, will have little difficulty in persuading them to raise the study of modern languages to the position which it should occupy in face of the urgent need of enthusiastic and fully qualified teachers.

But, more than in any other direction, its influence may be of the highest value in leading teachers to feel that they are, before everything else, servants of the nation, and in causing them to regard the social and economic conditions of their local surroundings

THE NATION'S OPPORTUNITY

in a new light, as forces moulding the national destiny. From experienced and varied study of American and foreign practice, it may bring to their notice the latest methods of teaching the mother tongue, history and literature, mathematics, science, and the other subjects which enter into the curriculum of a modern secondary school. Teachers themselves may be encouraged to go abroad to study and report on foreign systems—a course of procedure which has proved of such inestimable benefit to Germany. The knowledge thus acquired by Englishmen should be widely diffused by the department—free of cost—among all teachers and members of local authorities.

Furthermore, under such a central body there would no longer be any risk of that enormous waste of careful experiment which, owing to individual isolation, has been one of the most regrettable features of our past education. Not only would inspectors always be on the look-out for such experiments, and watch and encourage them, but it would be the duty of the department to register permanently the results obtained, and thus carefully mark each stage of the natural development of English education. By regularly diffusing the information collected in this manner it would do more than has ever been done to promote progress.

In spite of its being somewhat commonplace, no better simile has yet been drawn with reference to the new central authority than that of a telephone exchange, affording an easy means of communication between teachers, schools, and local authorities in all parts of the country. It must not forget, however, to "ring up" any persons who are not taking due advantage of the facilities afforded by the head office. And, to press this borrowed figure further, there must be an ample provision of trunk lines connecting the Primary, Secondary, and Technical Departments. For the efficiency of national education depends on the efficiency of each of these three branches.

It may be some time before such organisation is completed. Slow and cautious action may be the surest way of securing ultimate success, but, on the other hand, every year that sees the continuation of abuses represents a strengthening of the roots of error which threaten to undermine the whole imperial edifice. Individuals may ignore this fact; those who do can have no part in the new organisation, for its success depends before all else on the men who direct it. Will the right men be selected to build up the national system of education? To produce order out of chaos is still the task dearest to the minds of Englishmen; it is scarcely necessary to point to the great monument which we are raising in Egypt to our powers of organisation, to show that there is no lack of competent men, and no hesitation to use them for the work, if only its importance and difficulties are appreciated.

Above all, do not let us despise the men who have spent long years of their lives in fighting the battle of education in the schools themselves, against the overwhelming odds of professional and public indifference. For these are the men who may best help the Board of Education to bring to its task a spirit of tactful guidance, a willingness to combine the scientific study of education with the due consideration of facts and of the practical conditions of life; and who, more than any others, can help to promote a friendly interchange of experience among the most devoted, the most sensitive, and often the most wayward of national servants—schoolmasters, the educators of the rising generation of Englishmen.

PLYMOUTH
WILLIAM BRENDON AND SON
PRINTERS

For Product Safety Concerns and Information please contact our EU
representative GPSR@taylorandfrancis.com
Taylor & Francis Verlag GmbH, Kaufingerstraße 24, 80331 München, Germany

www.ingramcontent.com/pod-product-compliance
Lightning Source LLC
Chambersburg PA
CBHW070737230426
43669CB00014B/2482